SRI Scholastic Reading Inventory

Installation Guide

Enterprise Edition v1.0

www.scholastic.com/sri

Powered by SAM™

ENTERPRISE EDITION

Published by Scholastic Inc.

Printed in the U.S.A.

ISBN 0-439-74217-X

1 2 3 4 5 6 7 8 9 10 10 14 13 12 11 10 09 08 07 06

Table of Contents

INTRODUCTION

Welcome

Welcome to the ***Scholastic Reading Inventory Enterprise Edition Installation Guide***.
Use this guide to:

- install the ***SRI Enterprise Edition*** software.
- troubleshoot any technical issues that arise during installation or operation.

This guide also contains detailed information on data management including: importing and exporting student information, backing up the database, and aggregating data across multiple Scholastic Achievement Manager (**SAM**) installations.

What You Need to Get Started

Scholastic recommends the installation be done by your school or district's network and systems technician or a person with equivalent skills; however, the installation can be performed by anyone with the following:

- Physical access to network servers and classroom workstations.
- Network-level full **Administrator** rights.
- Permission to modify network settings and user privileges. This is controlled by your network administrator, as determined by school or district IT policies.

Schools and classes also need to be set up by someone with administrative privileges. This must be done before any students can be added. You can do this during the installation process or at a later time. For specific instructions see the section beginning on **page 62**.

Windows and Macintosh Platforms

Installation steps are essentially the same whether you are installing to a Windows or Macintosh platform. Any differences are noted in the text. For brevity, we show pictures of Windows screens only. Macintosh screens display slightly different button design, but all labels are the same.

Each file folder separator in this document is a Windows-style backslash. This has the same significance as the forward slash convention used for Macintosh OS X and colon convention for Macintosh Classic operating systems. This document presents file names, using uppercase and lowercase letters, as they are actually coded.

Scholastic Management System (SMS) to Scholastic Achievement Manager (SAM) Conversions

Users who are converting from an SMS installation (SMS v1.6 or SRI and SRC! 3.x) to a SAM installation will find some key differences between the two systems.

- SAM uses HTTP (Hypertext Transfer Protocol) for server/client communication.
- With improved reporting, SAM provides more tools for data-driven instruction.
- SAM has easy-to-use navigation with simple drill-down capabilities.

One of the most important points about converting from SMS to SAM is that it is possible to migrate your SMS data into the new SAM database. Detailed instructions for this procedure begin on **page 81**.

Important Note: If you plan to migrate data, it is **imperative** that:

1. No teachers sign in to SAM prior to Data Migration.
2. No students use any of the new Scholastic EE (Enterprise Edition) programs (**SRI, *READ 180*, Scholastic Reading Counts!, rSkills Tests, or *ReadAbout***) prior to Data Migration.

What's inside

This document provides:

- Scholastic's recommendations for best implementation practices. See SYSTEM COMPONENTS, REQUIREMENTS, AND CONFIGURATIONS, **page 9.**
- Steps for installing SAM and **SRI** on the server and workstations. See SERVER & CLIENT INSTALLATION, **page 17**.
- Instructions for migrating data from your existing **SRI**/SMS installation to your new **SRI** ***Enterprise Edition.*** See MIGRATING DATA FROM THE SMS, **page 81**.
- **SRI** troubleshooting. See TROUBLESHOOTING and FAQs, beginning on **page 142**.
- Contacts for help. See CONTACTS, **page 174**.

SYSTEM COMPONENTS, REQUIREMENTS, AND CONFIGURATIONS

Software Components

SRI ENTERPRISE EDITION

Application	Runs On	Accessed By
Scholastic Reading Inventory™ (SRI) assessment software	student workstations in *SRI* classroom(s) or reading labs; teacher workstations optional	students and teachers
Scholastic Achievement Manager™ (SAM) database management	administrative workstation, teacher workstation; student/teacher workstations optional	teachers, administrators, and technical administrators

SRI database management through SAM

Application	Runs On	Administered By
SAM Server	network server	School and SAM administrators; teachers (depending on permissions) **Note**: Do not share the Scholastic EE folder as connections are IP.

System Specifications

Recommended hardware and software requirements for servers and for student and teacher workstations:

Computer	*Platform*	*Operating System (with latest Service Packs)*	*Processor*	*Memory*	*Free Hard Disk Space*	*Other*	*Internet Access*
Student Workstation	Windows	Windows XP Pro SP2	Pentium IV/ 1.0 GHz	256 MB	500 MB*	QuickTime, 16-bit sound card, headphones, microphone, browser	No
	Macintosh	Mac OS X v10.4.x	G4/1.25 GHz				
Teacher or Administrator Workstation	Windows	Windows XP Pro SP2	Pentium IV/ 1.5 GHz	512 MB	500 MB	QuickTime, 16-bit sound card, Acrobat Reader, headphones, browser	Yes
	Macintosh	Mac OS X v10.4.x	G4/1.25 GHz				
Application Server	Windows	Windows 2003 Server	Dual 3.2 GHz Xeon	2048 MB	5 GB	The installer will configure the server with correct versions of MySQL, JBoss, and Java.	Yes
	Macintosh	Mac OS X v10.4.x	Dual 2.0 GHz G5				
Data Aggregation Server (Optional)	Windows	Windows 2003 Server	Dual 3.2 GHz Xeon	2048 MB	1 GB per school		Yes
	Macintosh	Mac OS X v10.4.x	Dual 2.0 GHz G5				

* SRI requires a minimum of 60 MB of free hard disk space.

Note: These technical requirements were accurate as of the date of print, 12/20/2005. Technical requirements change frequently as a result of new hardware and system software releases by Apple, Microsoft, Adobe and other companies. Please check the Scholastic Web site at ***www.scholastic.com/SRItechspecs*** for the very latest updates.

Compatible operating systems

Servers:

The Enterprise products have been certified to work on the following servers:

- Windows 2000 Server and Windows 2003 Server with PIII 800 or higher processor.
- Mac OS X v10.3.x and Mac OS X v10.4.x Servers with G5 or higher processor. Enterprise Edition programs on Mac OS X run in Native mode.

The following servers are **not** supported:

- Windows 98, ME, and NT
- Mac OS X Server v10.0–v10.2; Mac 9.2 Server
- Novell 4.x, 5.x, 6.x, and OES

Workstations:

The Enterprise products have been certified to work on the following workstations:

- Windows 98SE, Windows 2000 Professional, Windows XP Professional with PIII 800 or higher processor
- Mac OS v9.2.2, Mac OS X v10.2.8, Mac OS X v10.3.x, and Mac OS X v10.4.x with G4 or higher processor. Enterprise Edition programs on Mac OS X run in Native mode.

The following workstations are not supported:

- Windows 95, 98 1st Ed., CE, NT, ME, 2000 Home; XP Home
- Mac OS v8.0–v9.1, Mac OS X v10.0–v10.2.7

Compatible Internet Browsers:

The following Internet browsers are supported (required for performing certain administrative tasks involving data import and export):

- Windows, Internet Explorer 5.x, 6.x, and 7.x
- Mac OS 9, Internet Explorer 5.1
- Mac OS X, Safari 1.2

Additional requirements

- Overall system performance, including number of concurrent users, is affected by network bandwidth, server memory, processor speed, disk drive performance, and many other factors.

- Scholastic strongly recommends SAM be installed on a dedicated server that is not used by other applications. If SAM is installed on a server shared with other applications, overall system memory and disk space requirements will vary according to the needs of the other programs.

- SAM Servers require a fixed IP address. Setup and management of the DNS is the responsibility of the school administrator; Scholastic does not provide an automated solution for DNS. Student and Teacher workstations do not require a static IP address.

  Note: In DHCP environments, it may appear that your server has a static IP address when, in fact, it does not. This is because DHCP servers tend to provide the same IP address over and over again to the same computer. This is based on the internal hardware address of the machine, called a MAC address (no relation to Macintosh computers). In any event, if you cannot have a static IP address, you can configure your server with DHCP but you must specify a manual address.

- Workstations and servers require a Network Interface Card supporting TCP/IP. Wireless networks (802.11a or 802.11g) are supported but are limited to the bandwidth capacity of your wireless network.

- Color printers are recommended for servers and teacher workstations, but a black-and-white printer is sufficient for all reports.

- Student, teacher, and administrator workstations, application servers, and data aggregation servers all require a CD-ROM drive.

Technologies used in *SRI* Enterprise Edition

TECHNOLOGY	DESCRIPTION
MySQL	MySQL is an open-source relational database management system (RDBMS) that uses Structured Query Language (SQL), the most popular language for adding, accessing, and processing data in a database.
JBoss	JBoss (pronounced "Jay Boss") is an open-source, Java-based application server used by SAM to: • handle communication between the Client applications and the SAM Server. • access the data within the MySQL database. Because JBoss is Java based, it can be used on any operating system that supports Java.
Flash	Short for "Macromedia Flash." Flash is a software technology that provides rich graphic presentations on client machines and the ability to communicate efficiently with servers. Flash is used to create the SAM, SRI, SRC, rSkills Tests, and ReadAbout clients.
Java	An object-oriented programming language and technology framework that allows one set of code to run on multiple operating systems. Java is used to create the SAM Installers, and is the foundation used to run the JBoss Application Server. **JVM** (Java Virtual Machine) is a software "execution engine" that runs Java programs. JBoss, which is written in Java, runs within (on top of) a JVM, and the JVM runs within (on top of) an operating system. **JRE** (Java Runtime Environment) is a runtime environment for Java applications.
HTTP	Hyper Text Transfer Protocol—a protocol used for communication between client machines and a server. Most commonly used by Web browsers (Internet Explorer, Firefox, Netscape) to talk to Web servers. For SAM, HTTP is used to communicate (behind the scenes) between the Client Application and the SAM Server.
PDF	Portable Document Format (PDF) is a file format developed by Adobe Systems for representing documents in a manner that is independent of the original application software, hardware, and operating system used to create those documents. SAM uses PDF technology to display reports.

Network Configurations

SRI Enterprise Edition has a variety of deployment options. Based on SAM architecture, which utilizes HTTP for server/client communication, you can configure the system depending on which programs you are using and your school or district network setup.

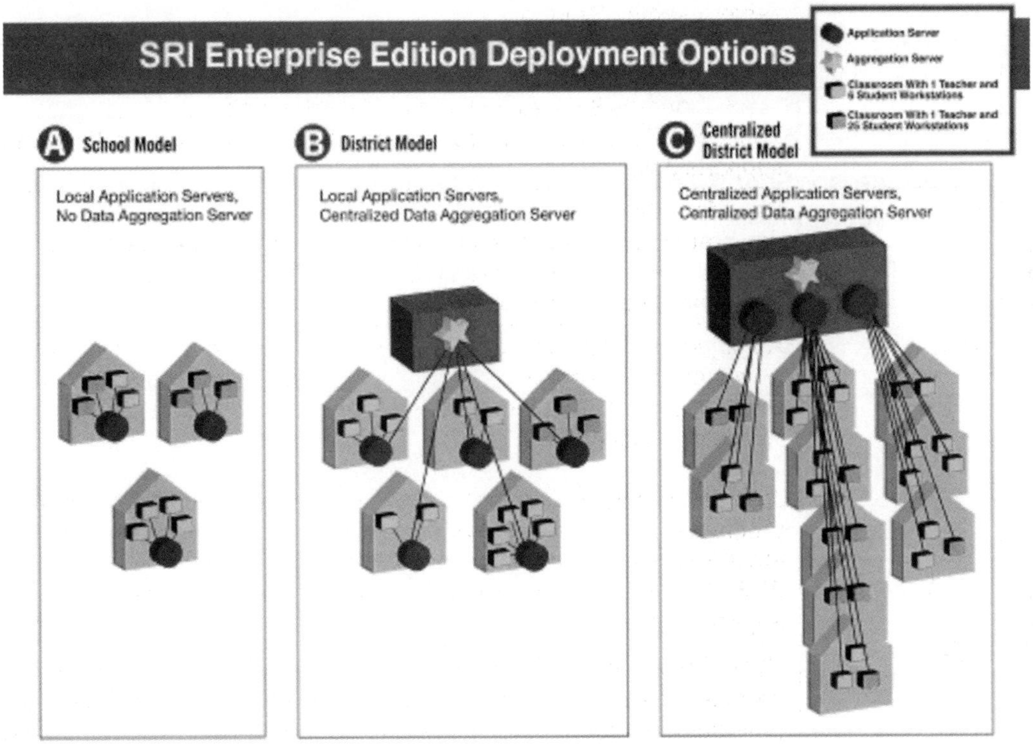

Factors that will affect program performance

Because ***SRI*** sends data and content between servers and workstations over a network, operating speed may be affected by:

Network factors:

1. Bandwidth—the theoretical maximum capacity of a network connection.
2. Bandwidth Utilization—the actual percentage of the bandwidth used.
3. Firewalls—security hardware and/or software that may be in place.

Hardware factors:

4. Processor Speed—how powerful your computer's processor is. Refer to the recommended requirements on **page 10**.
5. Available Memory—the amount of RAM available on your system. Refer to the recommended requirements on **page 10**.

SERVER & CLIENT INSTALLATION

Overview

Installing the ***SRI Enterprise Edition*** is a multistep process that includes installing software on a network server and on client or workstation computers in classrooms. During the installation process you will also provide the system with information that links the teacher and student workstations to the server.

> **Note:** If you have existing installations of Scholastic software, including ***Scholastic Reading Inventory, READ 180,*** or ***Scholastic Reading Counts!*** we recommend that you perform an SMS backup, which you save to a safe place, before installing the Enterprise Edition.

You will need 5 GB of free space on the server to install all ***SRI Enterprise Edition*** Server software. This includes 400 MB of pre-allocated space for the database. SAM will notify you if your database requires more space than is available on the server.

Order of Installation

The order of installation can vary, but we strongly recommend the following. Note that the SAM Server must be installed before the SRI Server.

1. **SAM Server:** This is the software that manages the Scholastic database and the communication between client computers and the server. It must be installed on the server designated for all of Scholastic's software.

2. **SAM Client:** This software is actually the interface that administrators and teachers will use when managing their districts, schools, classrooms, and students. The SAM Client should be installed on the SAM Server, and then may be installed on any other administrator or teacher computer.

3. ***SRI* Server Component:** The Scholastic program server components store information for and communicate with the program client software. Once SAM is installed, the server software for any Scholastic software you have purchased (for example **Scholastic Reading Inventory**, ***READ 180***, ***Scholastic Reading Counts!***) must be installed on the designated server.

4. **Student/Client Software:** This is the software that students will interact with, such as **Scholastic Reading Inventory** or ***Scholastic Reading Counts!***

You may also want to set up a **SAM Data Aggregation Server**. For information on this setup, please see the section that begins on **page 128.**

Follow the steps in the sections below to install all of the server and client software that comprises the ***SRI Enterprise Edition***.

SAM Server Installation

Overview

The SAM Server provides centralized storage for Scholastic programs and is where the Scholastic database resides. The SAM Server software incorporates several distinct software components that work behind the scenes to manage and store data generated by teachers and students using the software. These programs are included on the installation disc. They are:

- JBoss
- MySQL
- Java

Before beginning the SAM Server installation process, verify that you have both the SAM Server installation disc and the SAM Client installation disc. During installation you will also need to record the SAM Server IP address and port number so the Client applications can communicate with the servers. This information is identified during the SAM Server installation.

- SAM Server software requires 5 GB of space.
- Setting up SAM will take about one hour (which includes installation, setting up the district and school information, and activating licenses). Additional time will be required to set up student and teacher workstations, import student information, and set up accounts for teachers and classes.

The server installation process creates a folder at the root of the system drive called ScholasticEE, which includes essential or required elements for the SAM Server, including the services. It is important that you do not share or change the default rights to this folder.

To familiarize yourself with the folder structure that installation of Scholastic software will create, see Appendix B: FOLDER STRUCTURES on **page 158.**

If you are transitioning from an SMS installation to SAM, instructions for migrating data begin on **page 81**.

Installation Process

To begin installing:

1. **Insert Disc 1: SAM Server**

   At the computer designated as the SAM Server, insert Disc 1, SAM Server into the CD-ROM drive. An installation guide window will appear; click **Install SAM Server** to begin installation.

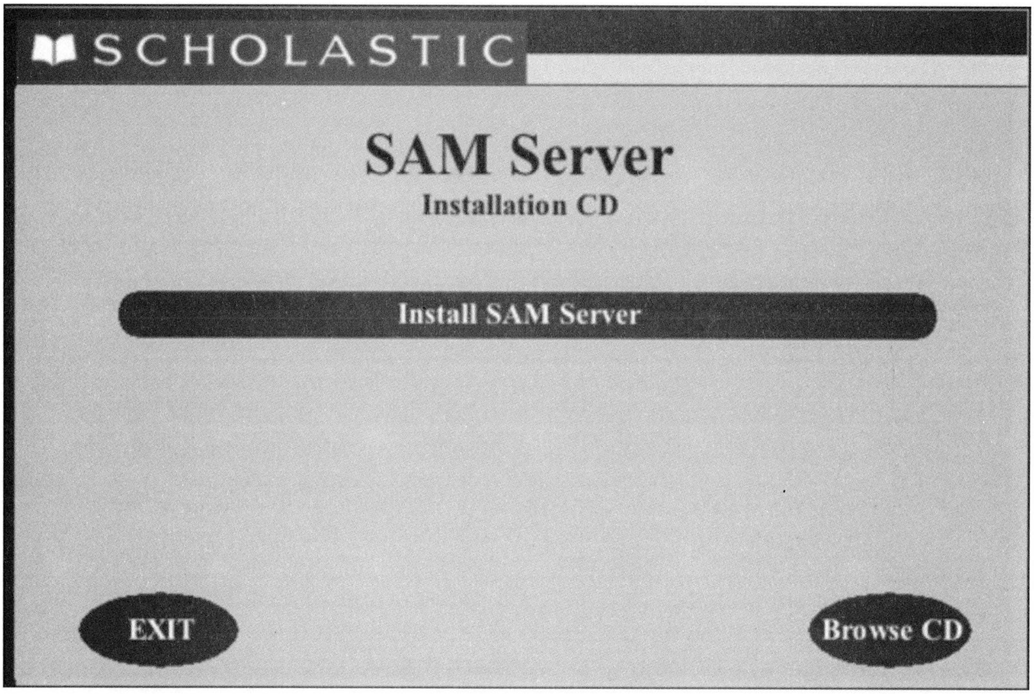

Mac Installation Note: On Mac servers double-click the Sam Server disk on the desktop, then double-click **Install**.

2. **Begin SAM Server Installation**

   The installation **Welcome** screen will display.

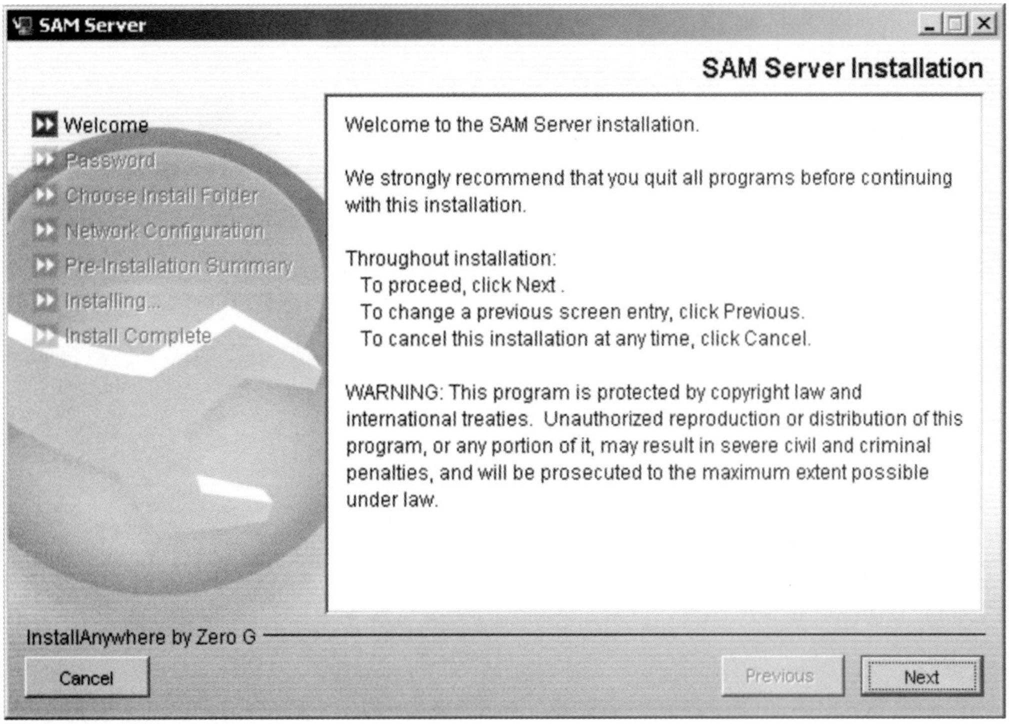

The files will automatically extract to begin the actual installation process. Instructions are displayed on the right side of the window, the left side of the window shows your progress through the installation.

As you move through the installation steps, you may:

- Click **Next** to proceed.
- Click **Previous** to return to a previous screen should you need to refer to the information or make a change.
- Click **Cancel** to exit the installation process at any time.

Click **Next** to proceed.

Mac Installation Note: If you are installing SAM Server on Mac OS X, you will see a screen that prompts you to enter the **Administrator Password** after the **Welcome** screen and before proceeding to the **Choose Install Folder** screen.

3. **Choose Install Folder**

   SAM will suggest the folder into which all of the server folders and files will be installed.

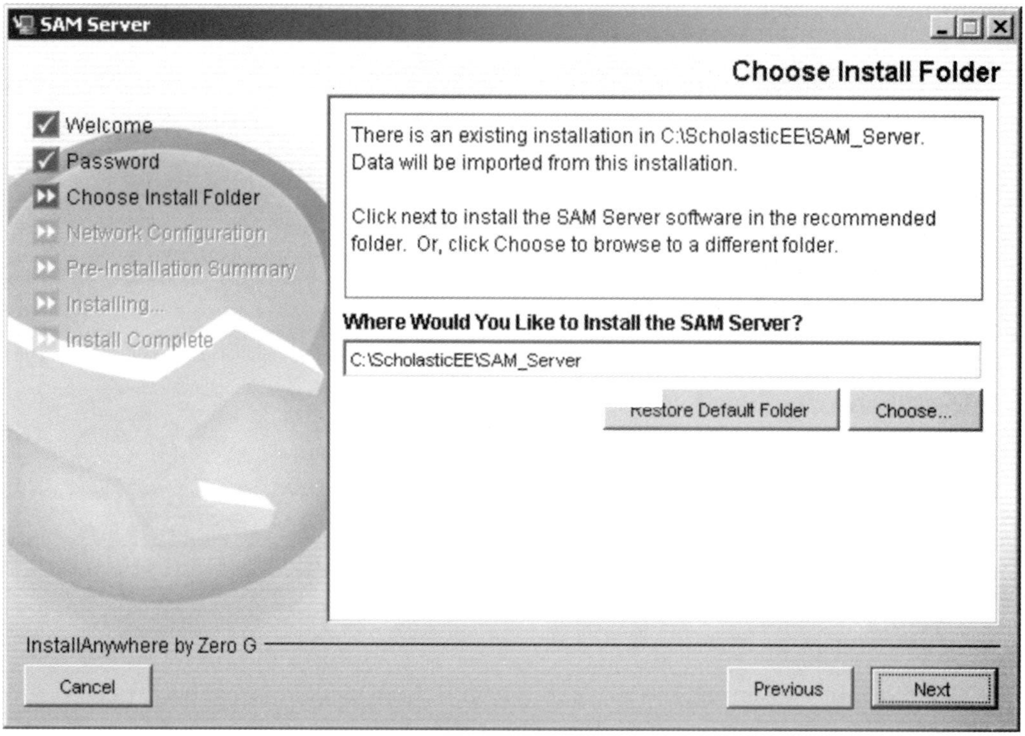

Use the **Choose** button to select a different folder. If you choose a different folder and decide not to use it, click the **Restore Default Folder** button. Click **Next** to continue.

4. **Network Configuration**

   IP Address: The system detects and displays your server's IP address, which is what will enable the client workstations to communicate with the server.

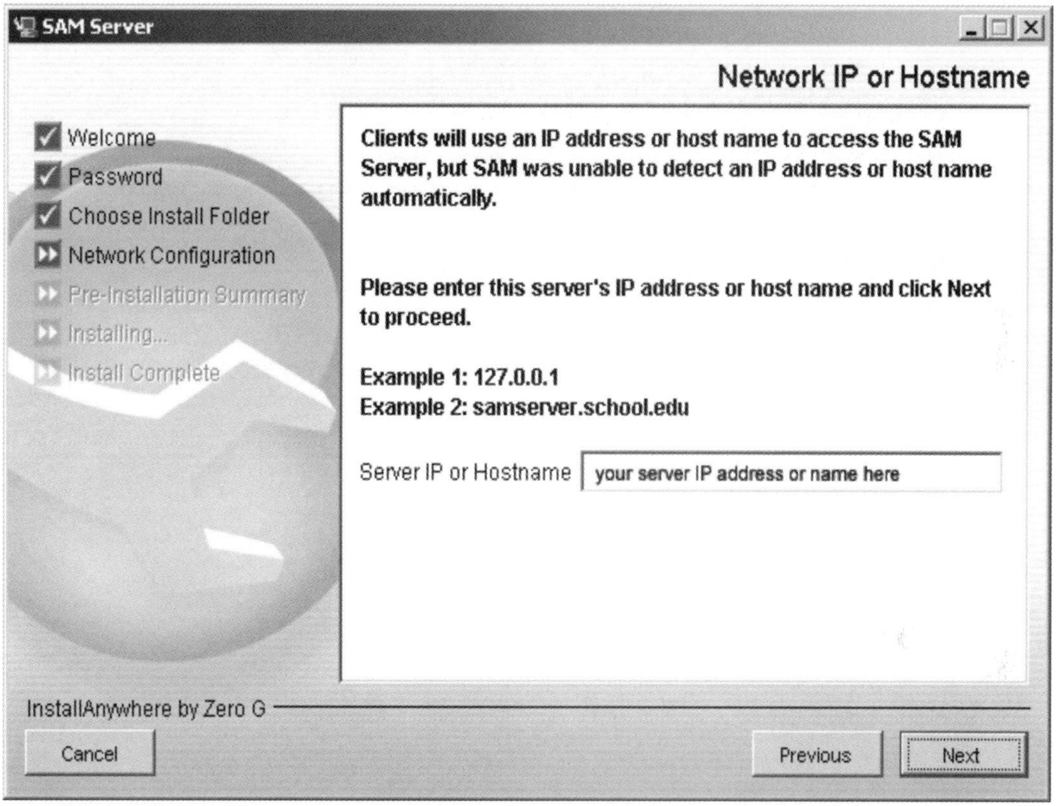

Note: The IP address shown above is an example. Your SAM Server IP address will be different.

To enter a different IP address, type it in the window. Be sure you enter the IP address **exactly** as it is displayed.

Click **Next** when the correct IP address is displayed.

5. **Port Configuration**

   The SAM Server communicates with the student and teacher workstations over the Internet or your school or district Intranet. SAM follows standard Internet protocols, using ports. You can find more information on standard port assignment in Appendix F on **page 169**.

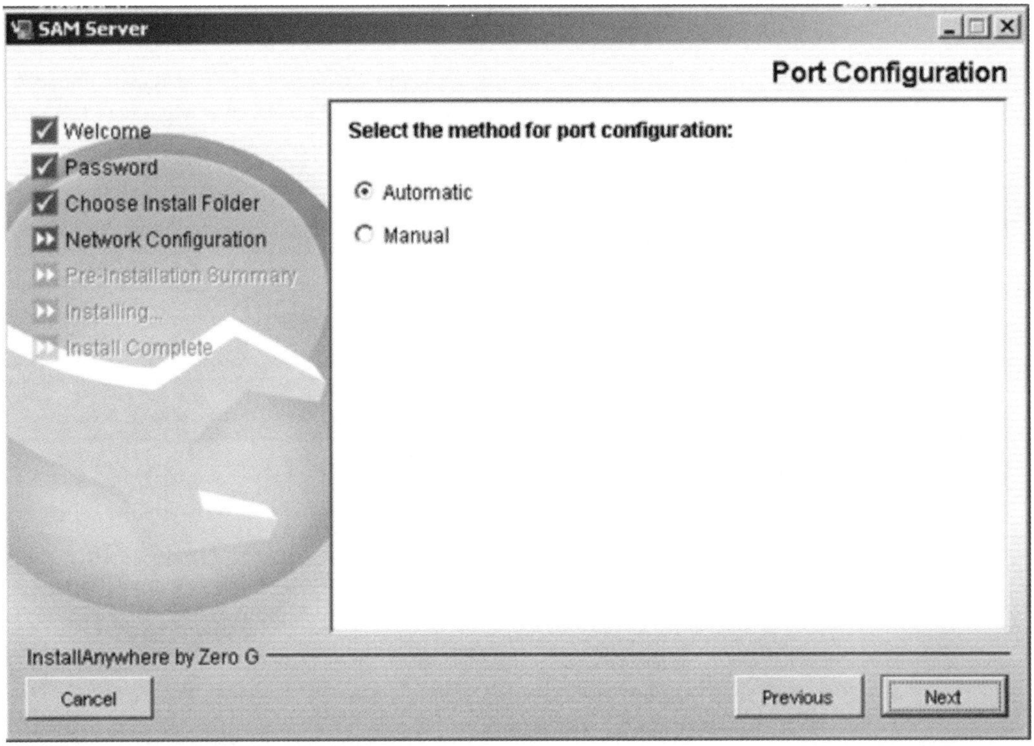

On the Port Configuration screen, use the radio button to select **Automatic** to allow the SAM installer to assign the ports. If you need to control port assignments, you may click **Manual** and use the next several screens to specify the ports to be used. Click **Next** to continue.

6. **Port Summary**

   If you have selected Automatic, the next window displays a list of the ports that SAM will use to interact with the workstations running the various Scholastic programs. You can find more information on standard port assignment in Appendix F on **page 169**.

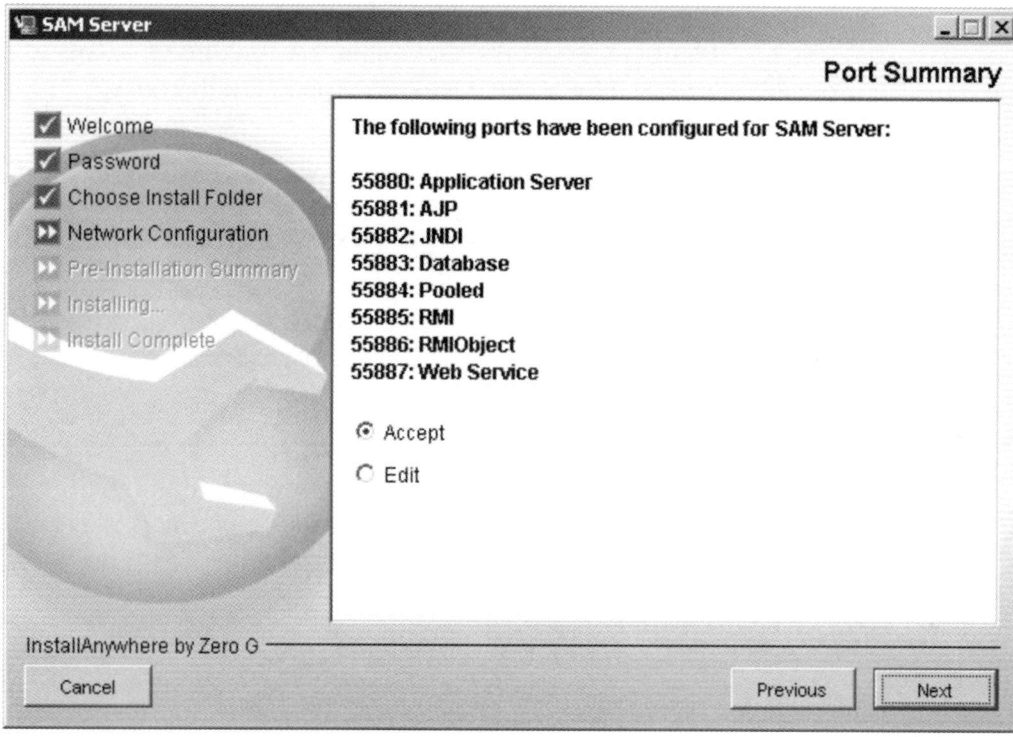

To accept the ports that SAM suggests, click the **Accept** radio button, then **Next**.

If you selected **Manual**, the next eight screens will allow you specify each port. At the completion of the port selection process, you will see this Port Summary screen. Click the **Edit** radio button to re-play the **Port Assignment** screens to change your choices. Or, click the **Accept** radio button if you are satisfied with port configuration, and **Next** to proceed.

The standard Application Server port number used for student and teacher workstations is 55880.

6a. Port Conflict Resolution and Individual Port Selection

You will be notified if there is a port conflict. SAM will make every effort to resolve a port conflict, though you may specify ports to be used, if you wish.

To specify ports, on the **Port Summary** window:

1. Click the **Edit** radio button. Then click the **Next** button.
2. You may change the port on each of the screens that follows, or simply accept it by clicking **Next** to proceed to the next screen.
3. When you have selected all of the ports, you will see a confirmation screen displaying the ports. Click **Next** to proceed and enter port numbers in the screens that follow.
4. When you have selected all of the ports, you will see the **Port Assignment Summary** screen displaying the ports. Click the radio button to **Accept** and click **Next** to proceed.

Note: If you are performing a reinstall of SAM Server, SAM will assign port 55882 as the new Application Server default port. To reset the port to 55880, you must **Edit** the port assignment screens and set the Application Server port to 55880, which is the port the clients are set to address.

7. **Pre-Installation Summary**

   This screen displays the system settings and resources necessary for the SAM Server installation. It's important to review this screen carefully—particularly the space requirements—so you can be sure you have adequate server space for the complete installation.

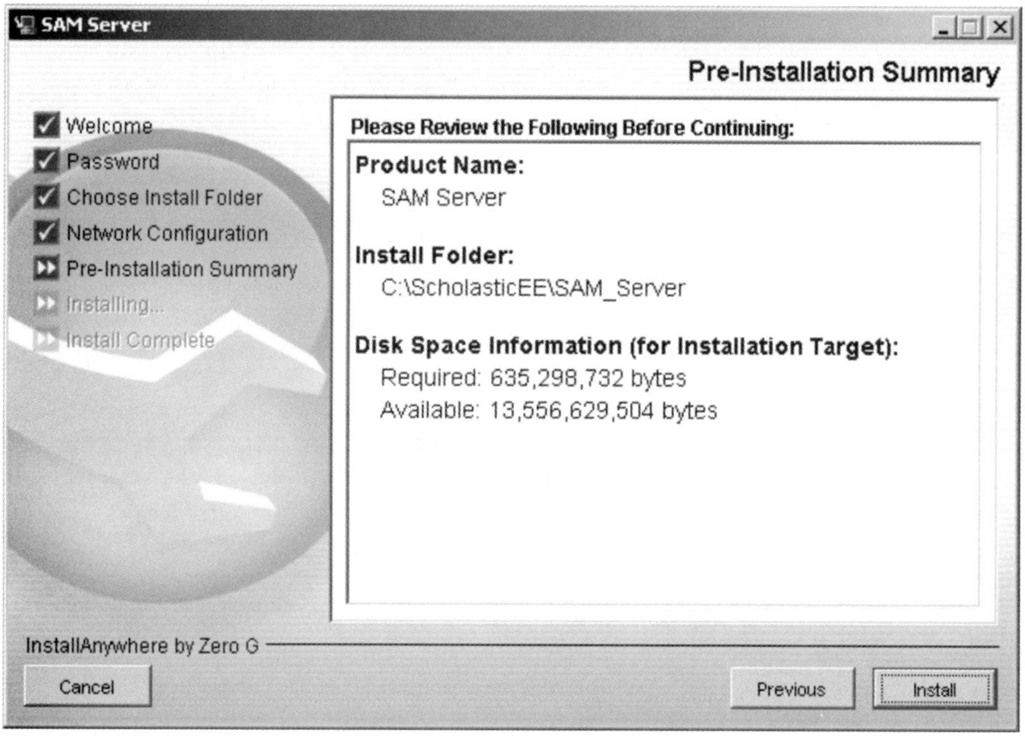

When you have reviewed all the information, click **Install** to proceed.

8. **Installation Progress**

   Once you click **Install** you will see the installation progress screen. You may stop the installation at any time by clicking **Cancel.**

   Note: Clicking **Cancel** may leave the SAM Server installation in an unstable state, which might cause difficulties should you try to install it again later.

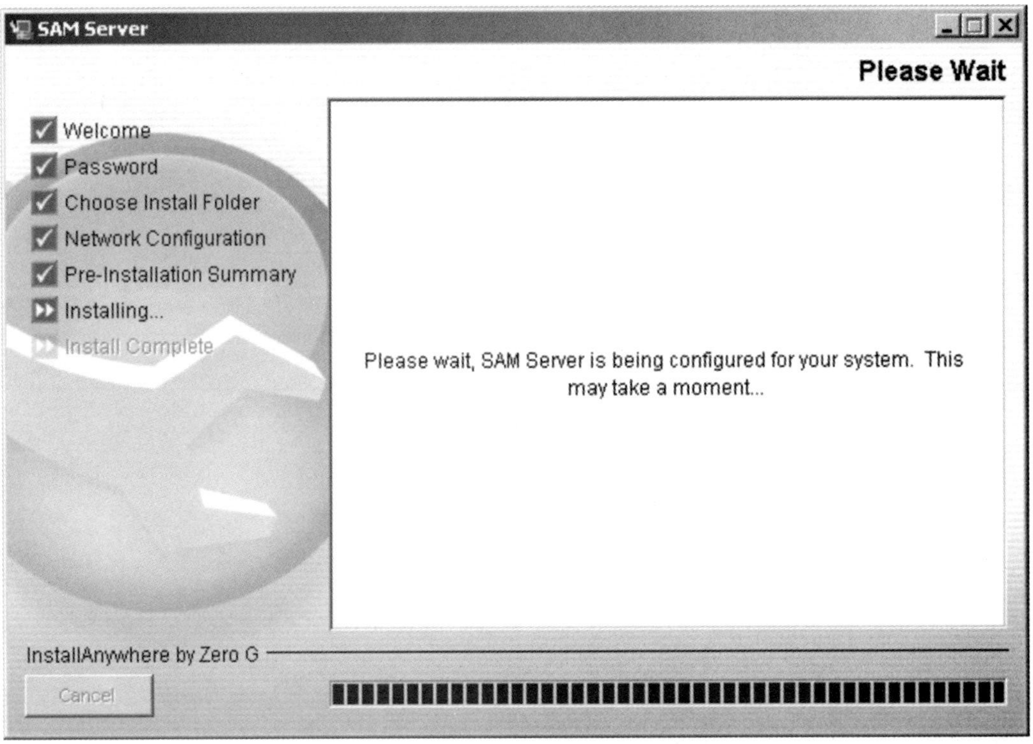

9. **SAM Server Install Complete**

   When installation is complete, SAM will display a screen summarizing important information about the Server installation. You will need the information from this screen for the installation of every Scholastic product that will be using SAM. Please be sure to record it below for future reference.

   - **Server IP address or host name** ________________
   - **Port number** ________________

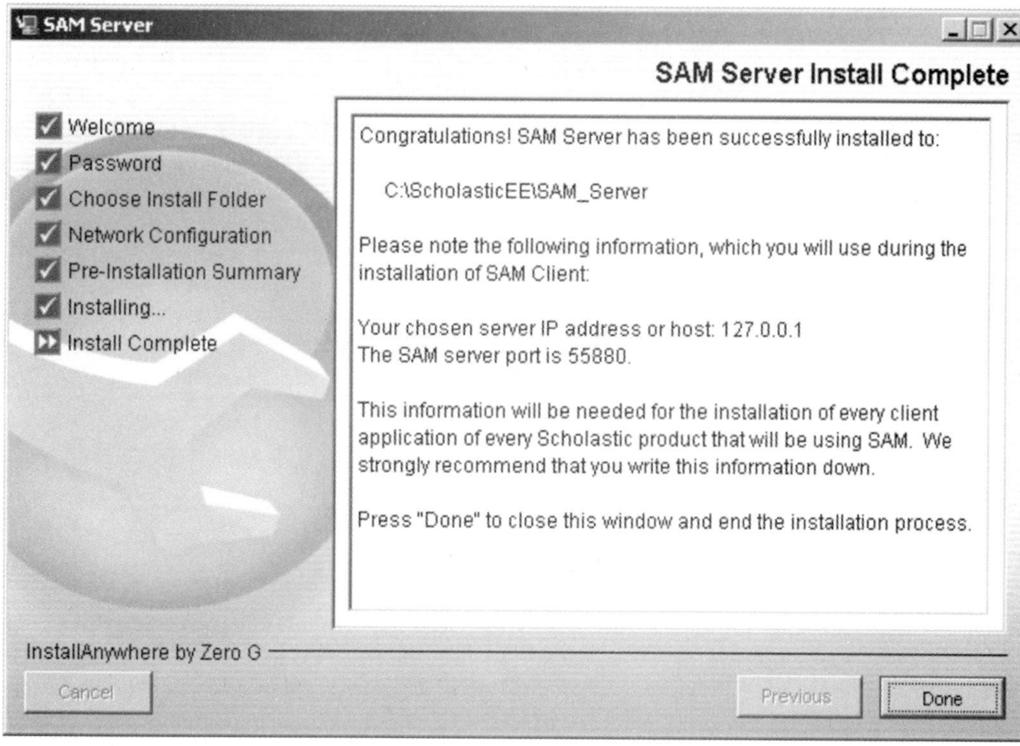

Note: The IP address and port number shown above are examples. Your SAM Server IP address will be different. Your port number may be the same or different.

Click **Done** when you have written down the above information to end the Server installation. The installation screen will close and you can proceed to SAM Client installation.

SAM Client Installation

Overview

The next step is to install the **SAM Client** on the computer that is the SAM Server. This will allow you to verify that the SAM Server installation was successful. If you are responsible for populating the database designated for Scholastic programs, you will use the SAM Client to set up the district, schools, teachers, and students who will be using Scholastic software.

Once you have signed in to SAM to verify that the SAM Server and SAM Client installations are working on the server, you must also install the SAM Client software on teacher workstation(s) that are accessible by teachers who will be using Scholastic software in their classrooms. The SAM Client is the software teachers will use to manage and grade students, run reports, and perform other day-to-day classroom management tasks.

You may install the SAM Client on the SAM Server, and/or on any computer that has a network connection and can communicate with the SAM Server.

Installation Process

To begin installing:

1. **Insert Disc 2: SAM Client**

   On the computer that is the SAM server, insert Disc 2 (SAM Client) into the CD-ROM drive. An installation guide window will appear; click **Install SAM Client** to begin installation.

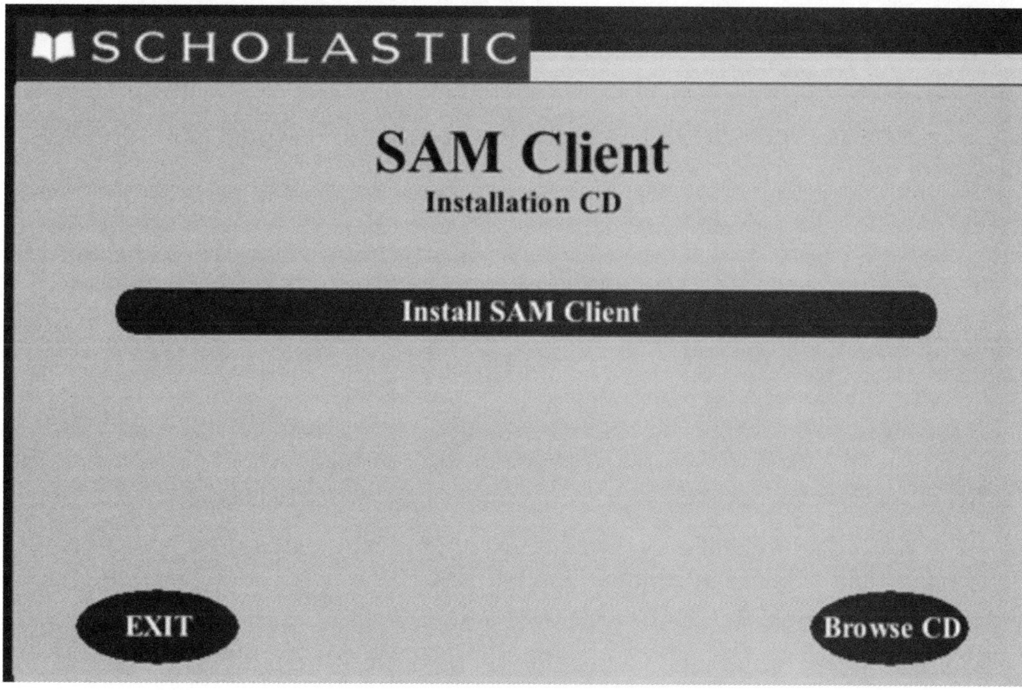

Mac Installation Note: On Mac servers double-click the **SAM Client** disk on the desktop, then double-click **Install**.

2. **Begin SAM Client Installation**

   The installation **Welcome** screen will display.

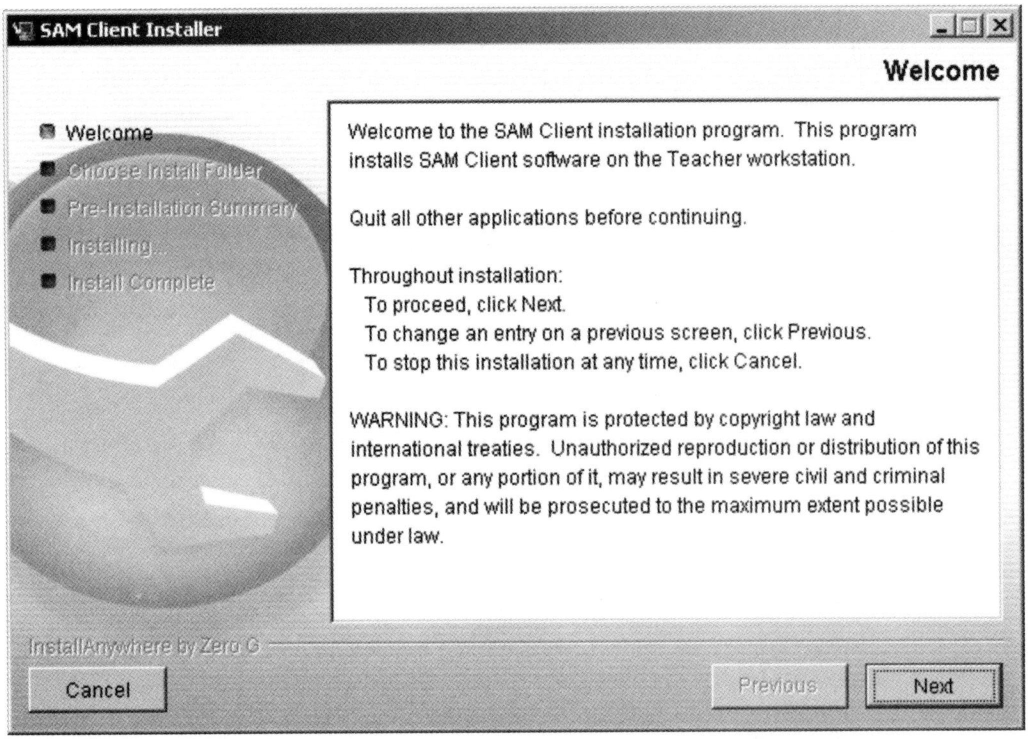

The SAM Client Installation Wizard will open. Instructions are displayed on the right side of the window; the left side of the window shows your progress through the installation process.

As you move through the installation process, you may:

- Click **Next** to proceed.
- Click **Previous** to return to a previous screen should you need to refer to the information or make a change.
- Click **Cancel** to exit the installation process at any time.

Click **Next** to proceed.

3. Choose Install Folder

SAM will suggest the folder into which all of the SAM Client folders and files will be installed.

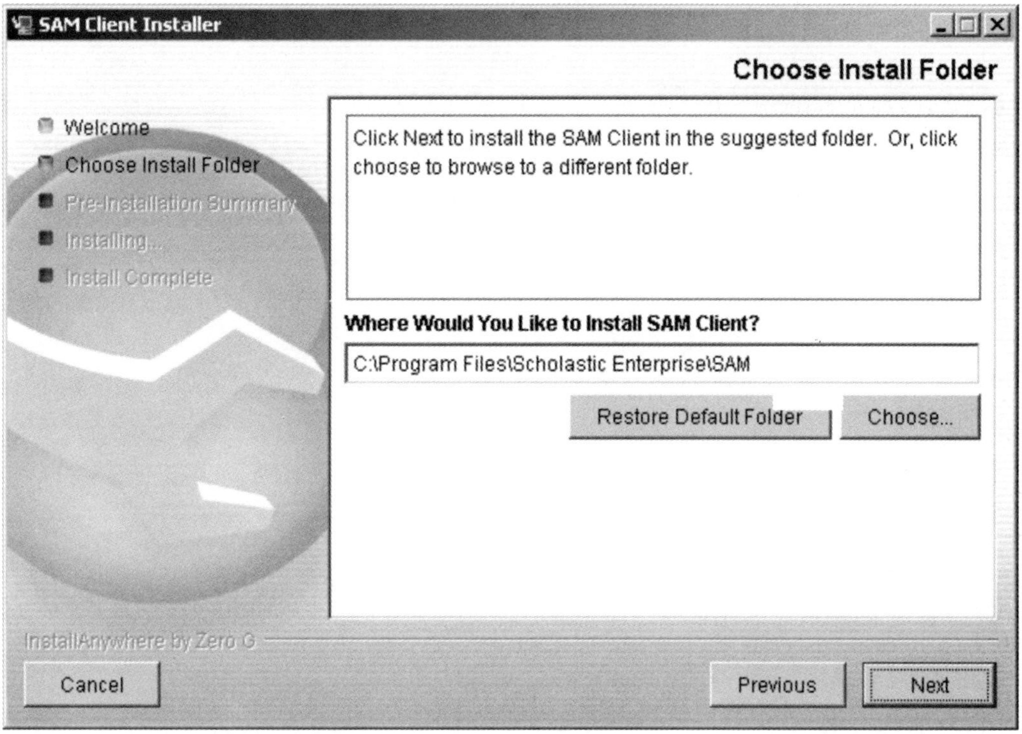

Use the **Choose** button to select a different folder. If you choose a different folder and decide not to use it, click the **Restore Default Folder** button.

Mac Installation Note: On Mac computers SAM will install in the Applications folder.

4. SAM Client Pre-Installation Summary

This screen displays the system settings and resources necessary for the SAM Client installation. It's important that you review this screen carefully—particularly the space requirements—to be sure you have adequate server space for the complete installation.

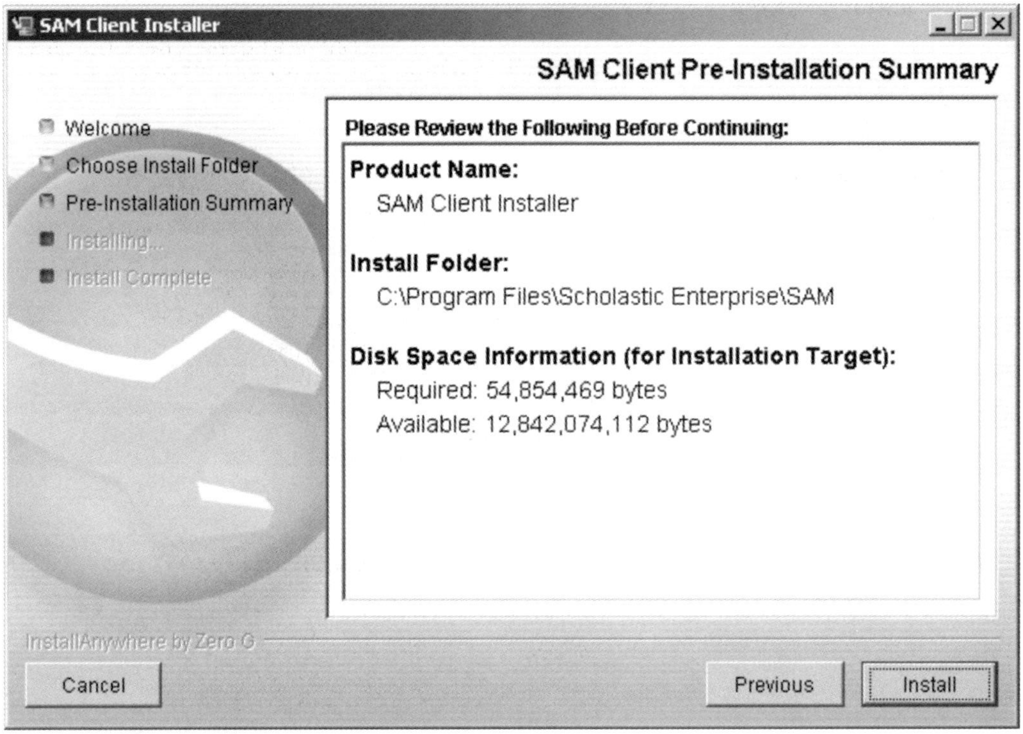

Once you have reviewed the information, click **Install** to proceed.

5. Installing SAM Client Installer

When you click **Install** you will see the **Installing SAM Client Installer** progress screen. You may stop the installation at any time by clicking **Cancel**.

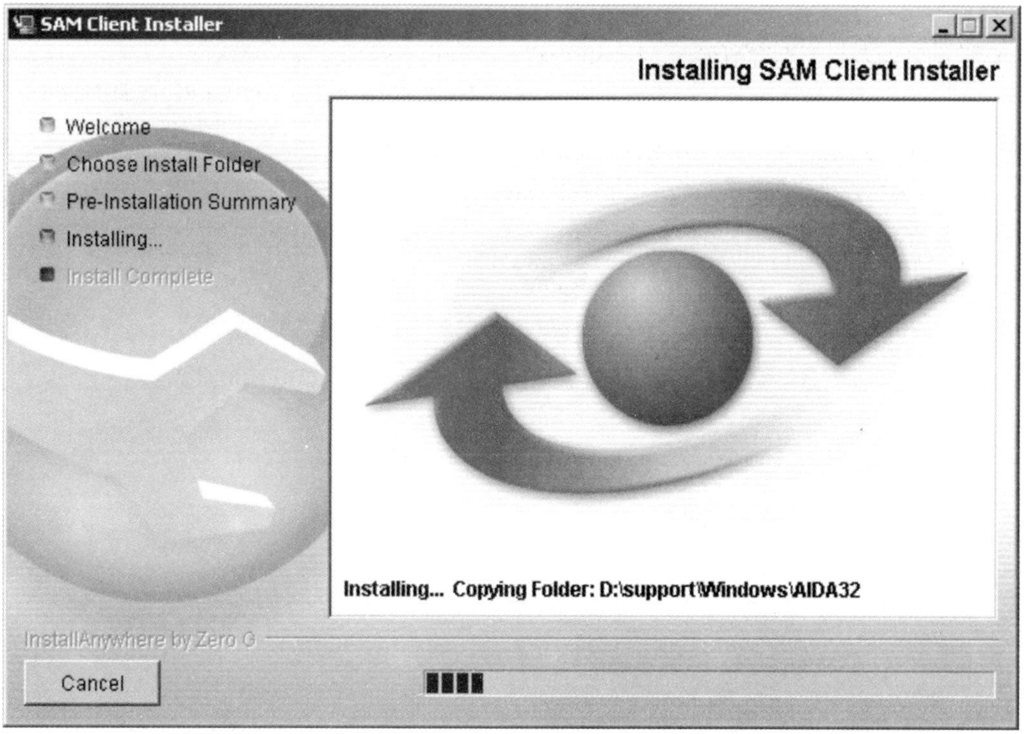

6. SAM Client Install Complete

Once all the SAM Client files are installed, the **SAM Client Install Complete** screen will display. Click **Done** to end the SAM Client installation process.

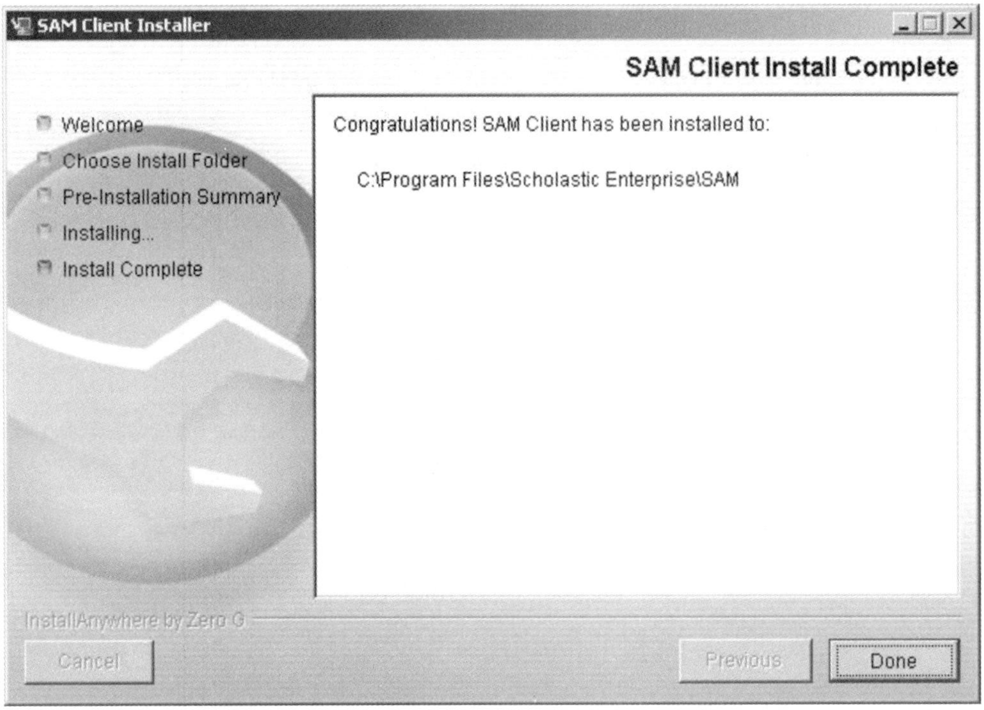

The Installation window will close and the SAM icon will be visible on your desktop. 

Verifying Success of SAM Server and Client Installation

To verify that the installation of both the SAM Server and the SAM Client software was successful, sign in to SAM using the following steps.

Double-click the SAM icon on your desktop to launch SAM.

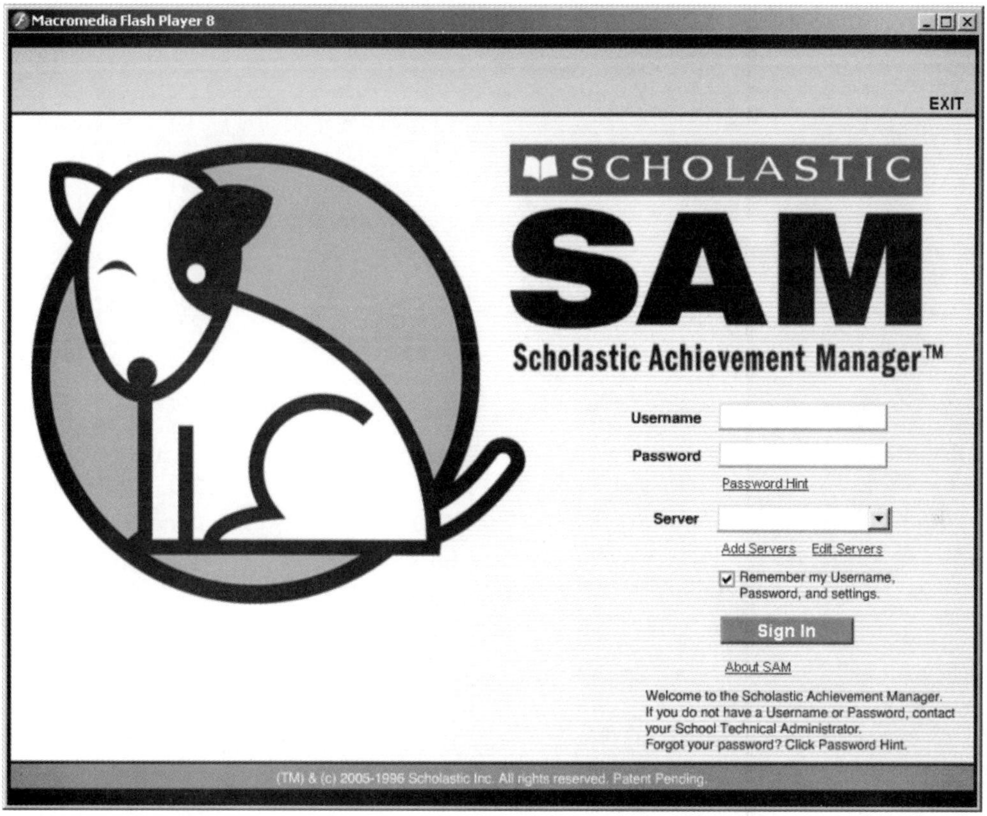

Adding a Server

To make the connection between the each SAM Client and the SAM Server, you must use the **Add Servers** link.

To add a connection to a SAM Server:

1. Double-click the SAM icon on your desktop to open the SAM Sign In window.

2. Click the **Add Servers** link. The **Add Server** window will open.

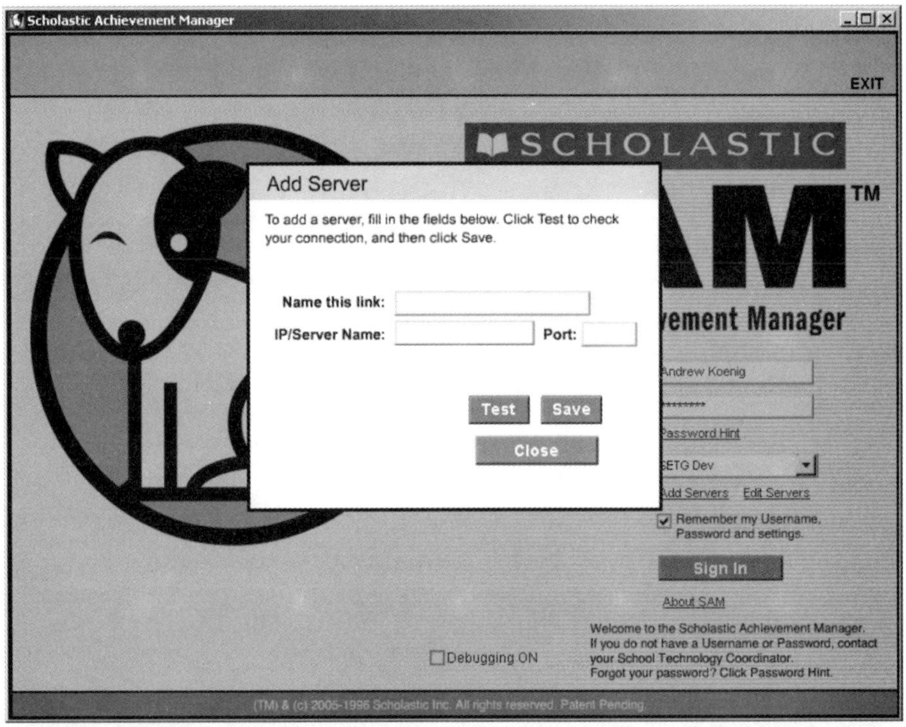

3. Enter a bookmark name in the **Name this link** field to describe the SAM Server, such as LINCOLN SCHOOL SERVER. If you enter a bookmark name that already exists, the system will notify you and you must change the name for one of the bookmarks.

4. Enter the SAM Server IP address and the port number as noted from the SAM Server installation process (See **page 29**). The default port is 55880.

5. Test the connection to the server by clicking **Test**.
   - If the test is successful, the system will notify you momentarily with a **Test Succeeded** notice.
   - If you receive a **Test Failed** notice, verify the SAM Server IP address and reenter it. If you are unable to create a domain for the SAM Server, contact Technical Support at 1-800-283-5974.

6. Click **Save** to close the **Add Server** window and return to the SAM Sign In screen.

Signing in to SAM for the First Time

To allow administrators to log in to SAM for the first time, a temporary username and password have been created. The username is **dadmin** and the password is **@dm1n**. You will use this temporary account to set up your SAM administrator profile.

Once you have created a link to a server, on the **Sign In** window:

1. Enter "dadmin" in the **Username** field.
2. Enter "@dm1n" in the **Password** field.
3. Click **Login**. The district administrator **Home Page** will open.

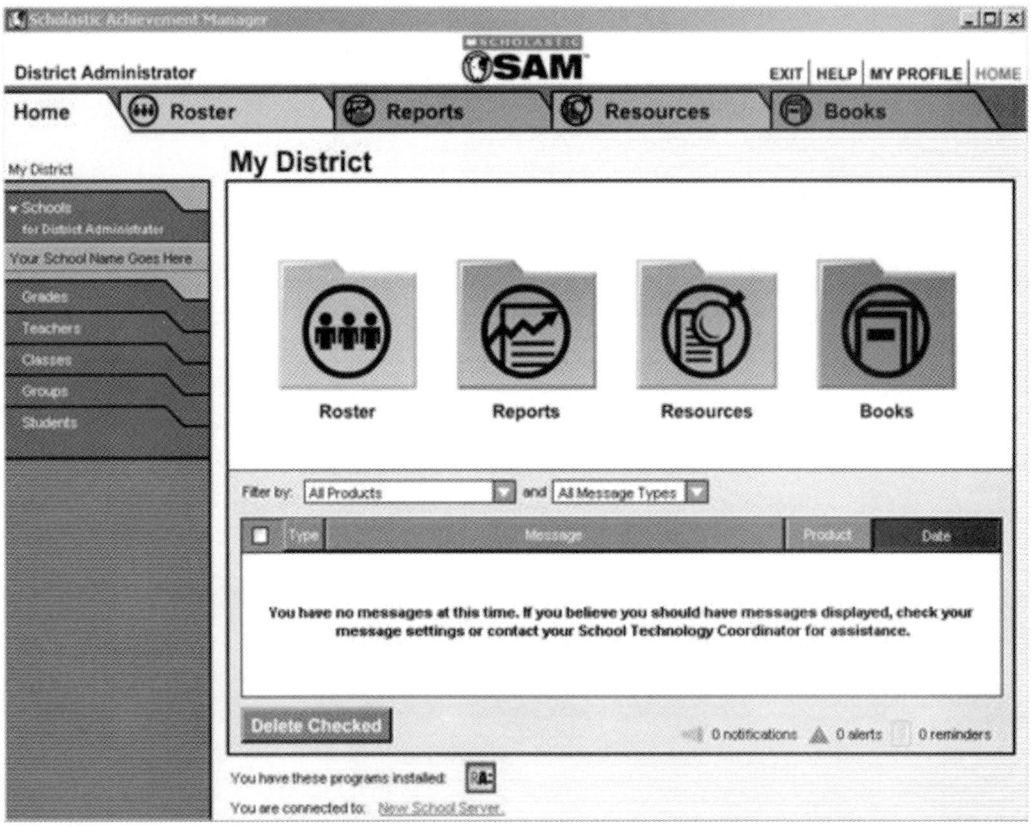

Changing your Username and Password

To maintain proper security measures for SAM, it's important to change your username and password immediately. To do so:

1. Click the **My Profile** link in the upper right corner of the home page. The **Edit District Administrator Profile** window will open.

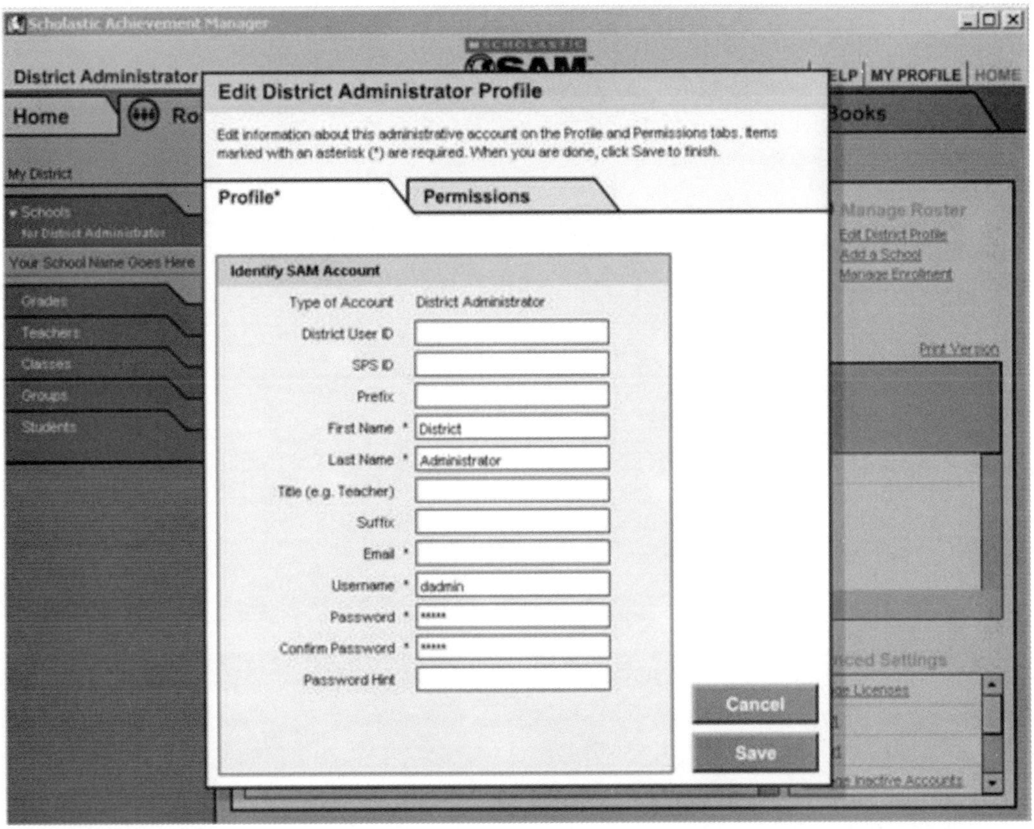

2. Enter the information on the **Edit Profile** window to reflect your contact information and preferences. **(Items with an asterisk [*] are required.)** When you are done, click **Save** to close the **Edit Profile** window and return to your **Home Page**.

The next time you sign in to SAM, use your selected username and password.

SAM Client Teacher Workstation Installation

Once you have verified that the SAM Server and SAM Client installations are successful, you must install the SAM client on the teacher workstations in your network. You will do this by following steps outlined above for Installation (beginning on **page 30**) and for adding a server (beginning on **page 38**).

The SAM Client installation on teacher workstations may be done next, or it can be done in conjunction with the installation of the ***SRI*** Client installations as you move from classroom to classroom.

As you install SAM Client on teacher workstations, be sure to create the connection to the SAM server (see Adding a Server on **page 38**) or, at a minimum, provide teachers with the server IP address and port number so they can make the connection.

You will also need to provide teachers with their username and password so they can sign in the first time.

SRI Server Installation

Overview

The ***SRI Enterprise Edition*** Server disk contains all of the server software needed to install the **Scholastic Reading Inventory** Server component.

Installation Process

On the school or district SAM server machine that will be running ***SRI***, sign in as a network administrator.

Quit all other applications running on the server that will be running ***SRI***. Make sure that all networked workstations do not have any Scholastic applications running.

To begin installing:

1. **Insert Disc 3: *SRI* Server**.

   At the computer designated as the ***SRI*** Server (which must be the same as the SAM Server):

   - Insert ***SRI*** Server disc into the CD-ROM drive. An installation guide window will appear.
   - Click **Install *Scholastic Reading Inventory* (SRI) Server** to begin installation of the ***SRI*** Server components.

Mac Installation Note: On Mac servers double-click the **SRI Server** disk on the desktop, then double-click **Install**.

Note: If you plan to use the Book Expert in SAM, you will need to install the **SRC! Book Expert Server** component. (It is not necessary to install the SRC! Client component.) You can do this at the end of the SRI Server Component installation, using the same disc.

2. Begin *SRI* Server Installation

The installation **Welcome** screen will display.

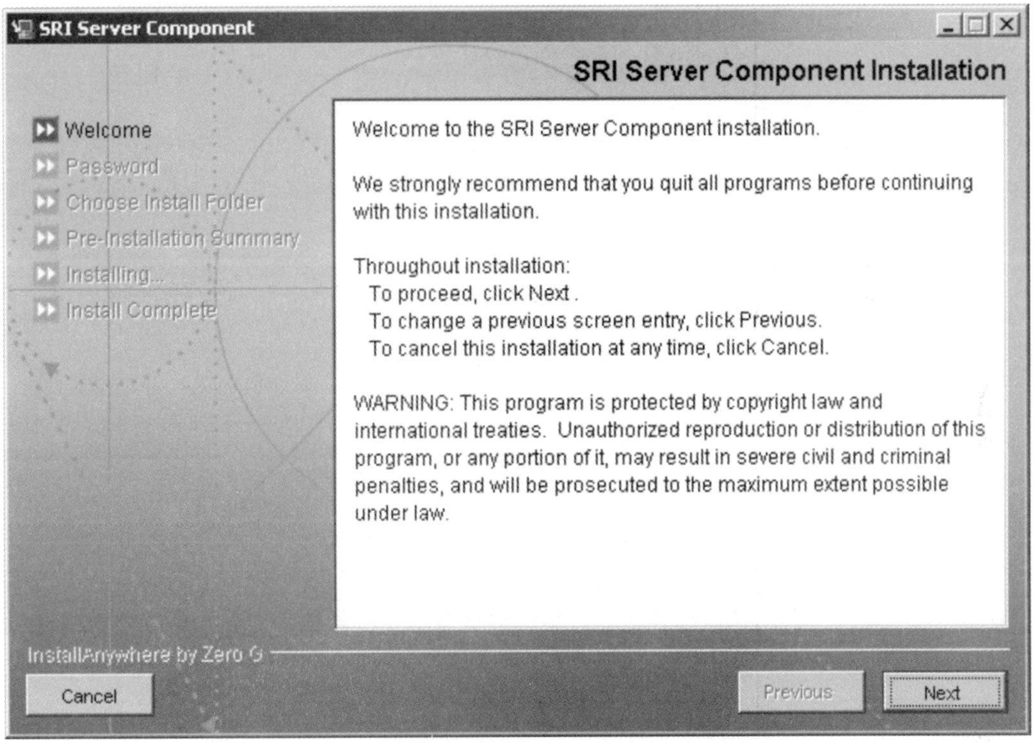

The files will automatically extract and a ***SRI*** **Server Component Installation** window will open. Instructions are displayed on the right side of the window; the left side of the window shows your progress through the installation process.

> **Note:** If the install program does not automatically launch, on the Windows Start menu, click **Run**, navigate to the CD-ROM drive, and at the top level of the ***SRI*** Installer CD click on the **Install** entry.

As you move through the installation process, you may:

- Click **Next** to proceed.
- Click **Previous** to return to a previous screen should you need to refer to the information or make a change.
- Click **Cancel** to exit the installation process at any time.

Click **Next** to proceed.

Mac OS X v10.4.x will ask for the administrator password after the welcome screen.

3. Choose Install Folder

The ***SRI*** Installer will suggest the folder into which all of the server folders and files will be installed.

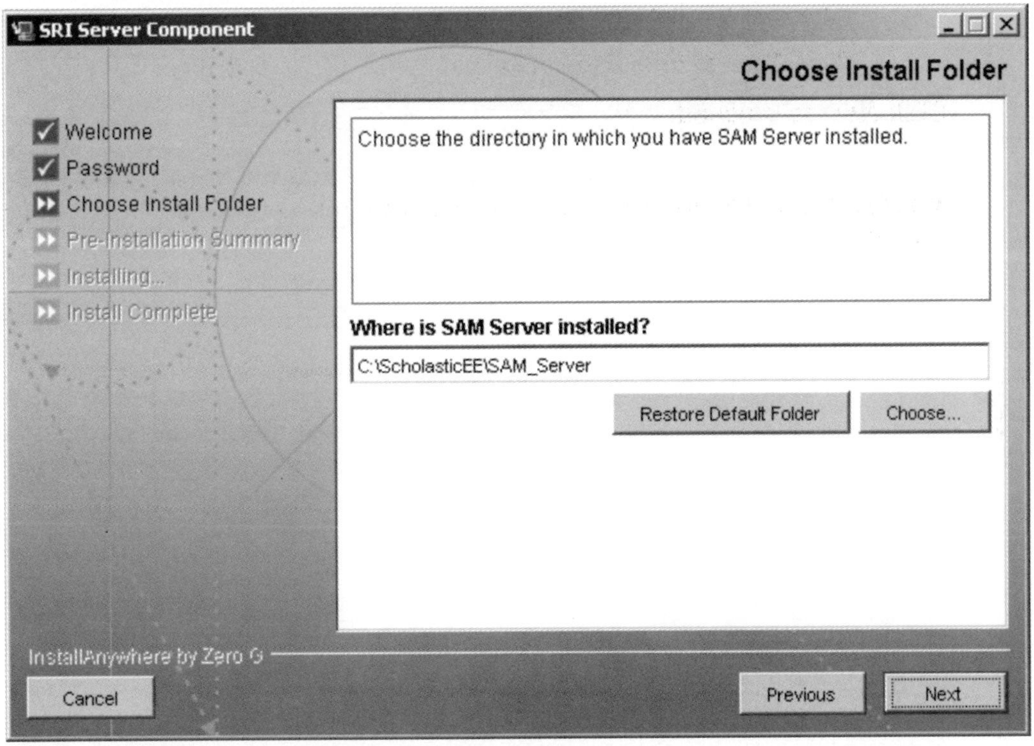

Use the **Choose** button to select a different folder. If you choose a different folder and decide not to use it, click the **Restore Default Folder** button.

Click **Next** to proceed.

4. Pre-Installation Summary

This screen displays the system settings and resources necessary for the ***SRI*** Server installation. It's important to review this screen carefully—particularly the space requirements—so you can be sure you have adequate server space for the complete installation.

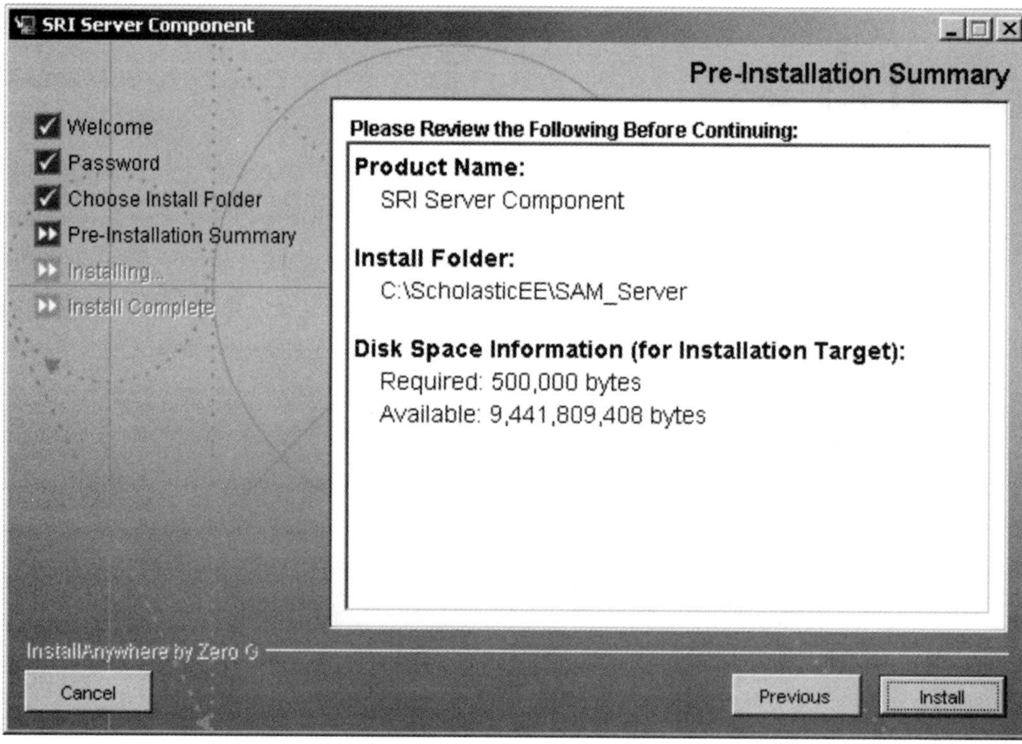

Click **Install** to proceed.

5. Installation Progress

When you click **Install** you will see the installation progress screen. You may stop the installation at any time by clicking **Cancel**.

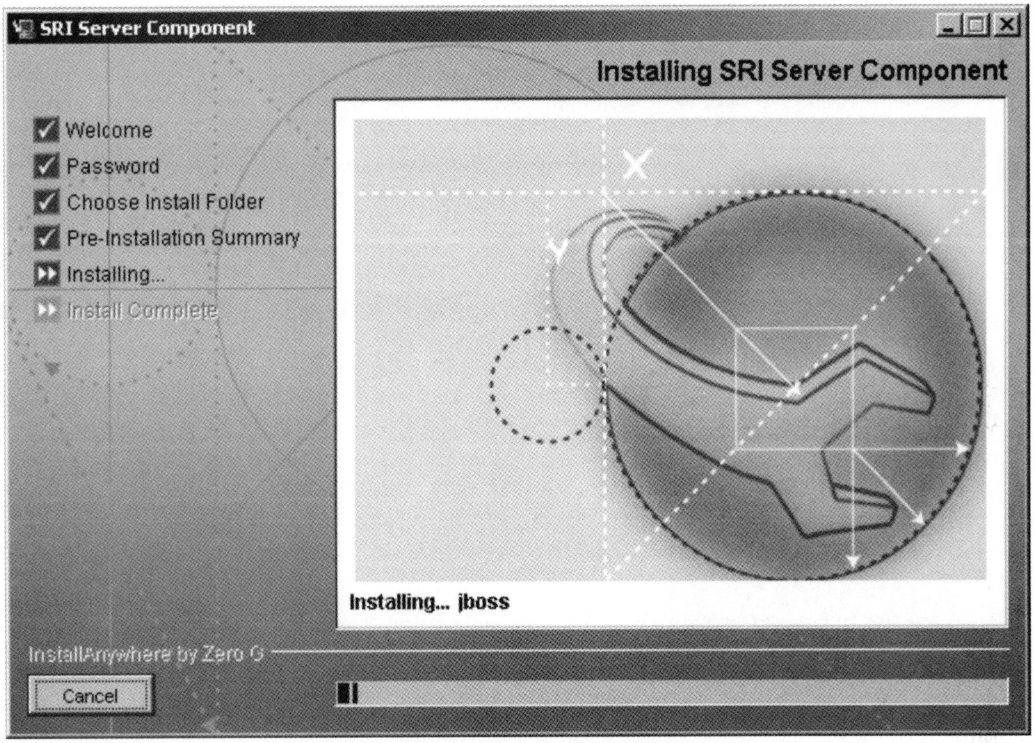

6. *SRI* Server Install Complete

Once all of the ***SRI*** Server files are installed, the ***SRI* Server Install Complete** screen will display. Click **Done** to end the ***SRI*** Server installation process and close the installation window.

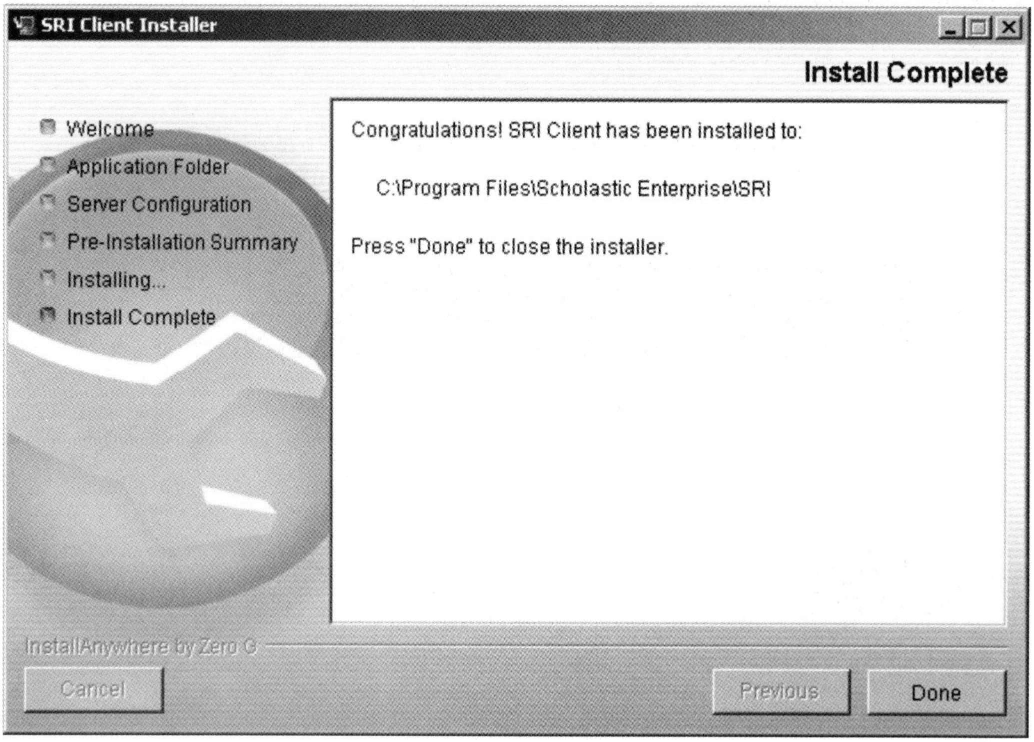

Note: If you plan to use the Book Expert in SAM, you will need to install the SRC! Book Expert Server component. (It is not necessary to install the SRC! Client component.)

To install the SRC! Book Expert Server Component:

1. Once you have completed the SRI Server Component installation, use the same disc to display the first screen. Click the **Start** button, select **Run**, then **Browse** to view the disc and select **install.exe**.

2. Click the **Install SRC! Book Expert Server** button.

3. Follow the instructions on the screens for the installation process; they are the same as the SRI Server Component installation screens.

4. Once you reach the SRC! Book Expert Server congratulations screen, you may move on to installing the SRI Client component, as described in the next section.

You will not need to install any SRC! Client component software to be able to access the Book Expert in SAM.

SRI Client Installation

Overview

The ***SRI*** Client contains the software students will use as they work in the program. You must use this CD to install the ***SRI*** Client on every student workstation on the network.

Note: Installation must be done directly from the disc in the CD-ROM drive. Installing over the network will not be successful.

Installation Process

To begin installing:

1. **Insert Disc 4: *SRI* Client**

At each workstation that students will use to run Scholastic programs, insert Disc 4 (***SRI*** Client) into the CD-ROM drive. An installation guide window will appear; click **Install Scholastic Reading Inventory Client** to begin installation.

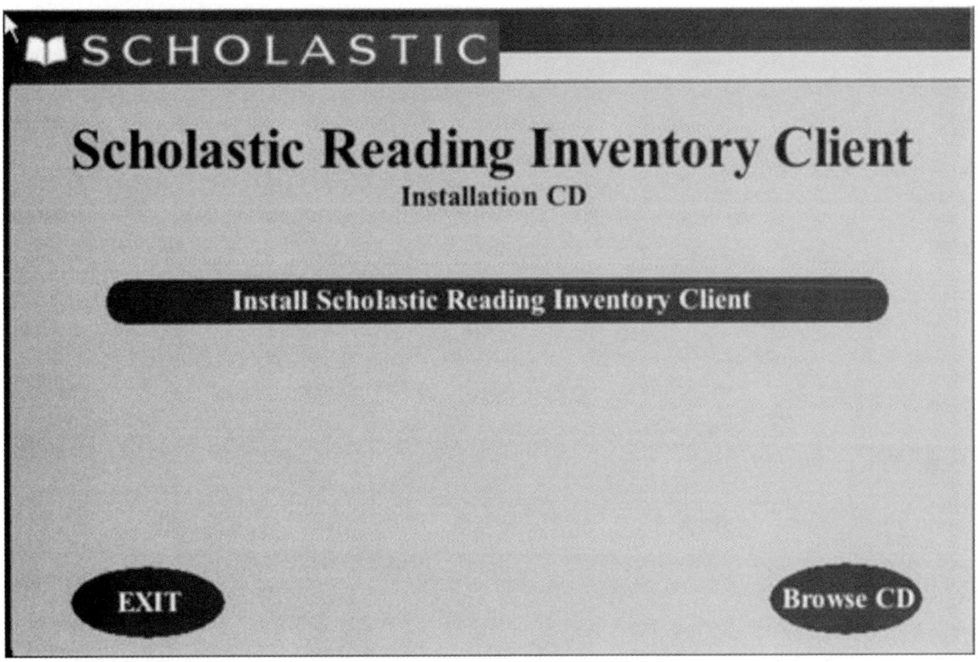

The ***SRI*** Client Installation Wizard will open.

Mac Installation Note: On Mac servers double-click the **SRI Enterprise Edition** disk on the desktop, then double-click **Install**.

2. **Begin *SRI* Client Installation**

   The installation **Welcome** screen will display.

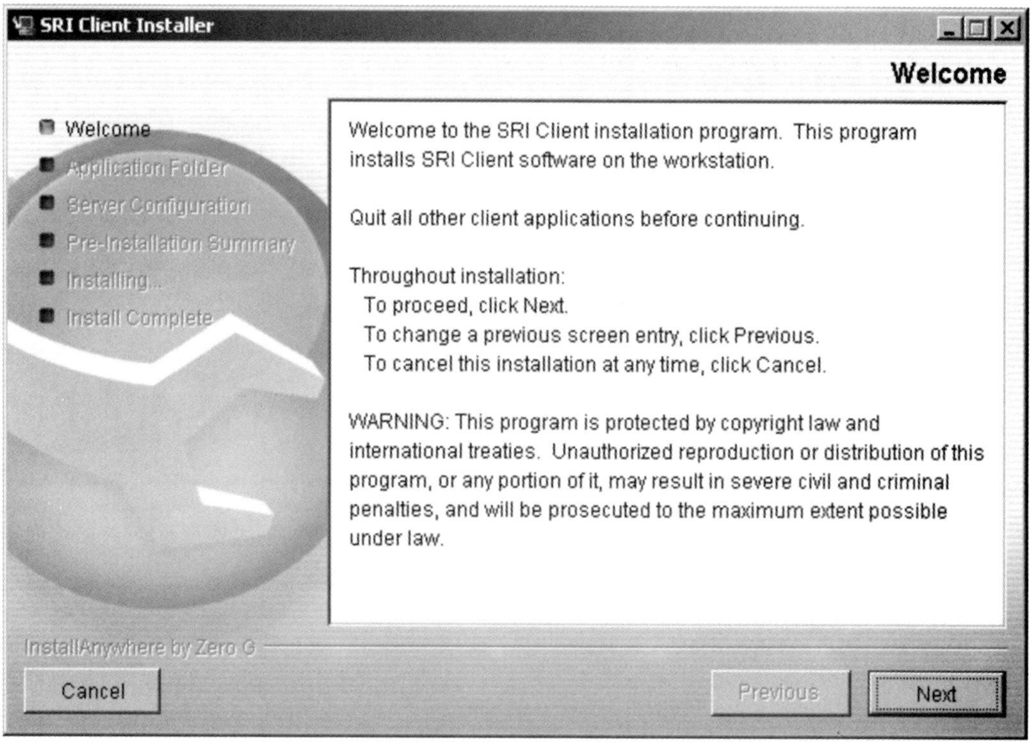

Instructions are displayed on the right side of the window; the left side of the window shows your progress through the installation process.

As you move through the installation process, you may:

- Click **Next** to proceed.
- Click **Previous** to return to a previous screen should you need to refer to the information or make a change.
- Click **Cancel** to exit the installation process at any time.

Click **Next** to proceed.

3. **Choose Application Folder**
   SAM will suggest the folder into which all of the ***SRI*** Client folders and files will be installed.

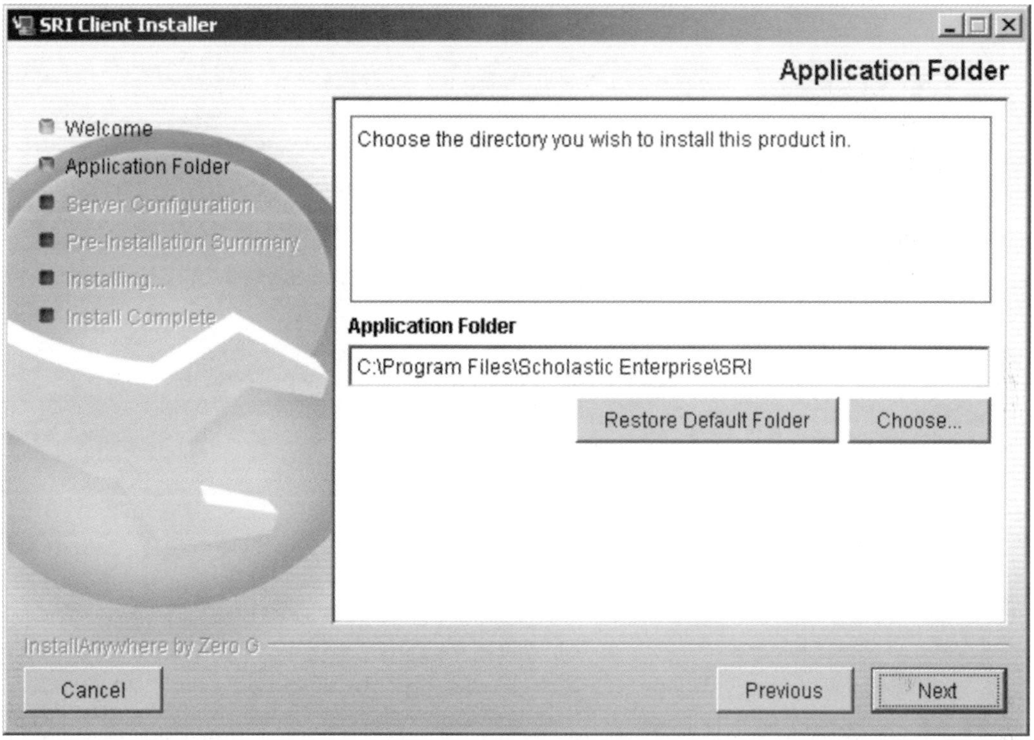

Use the **Choose** button to select a different folder. If you choose a different folder and decide not to use it, click the **Restore Default Folder** button.

Mac OS X workstations will install in the **Applications** folder.

Click **Next** to proceed.

4. **Server Configuration**

   Enter the SAM Server IP address and Server port, which were determined during the SAM Server installation. (See **page 29**.) For instructions on locating the server IP address, see **page 150**.

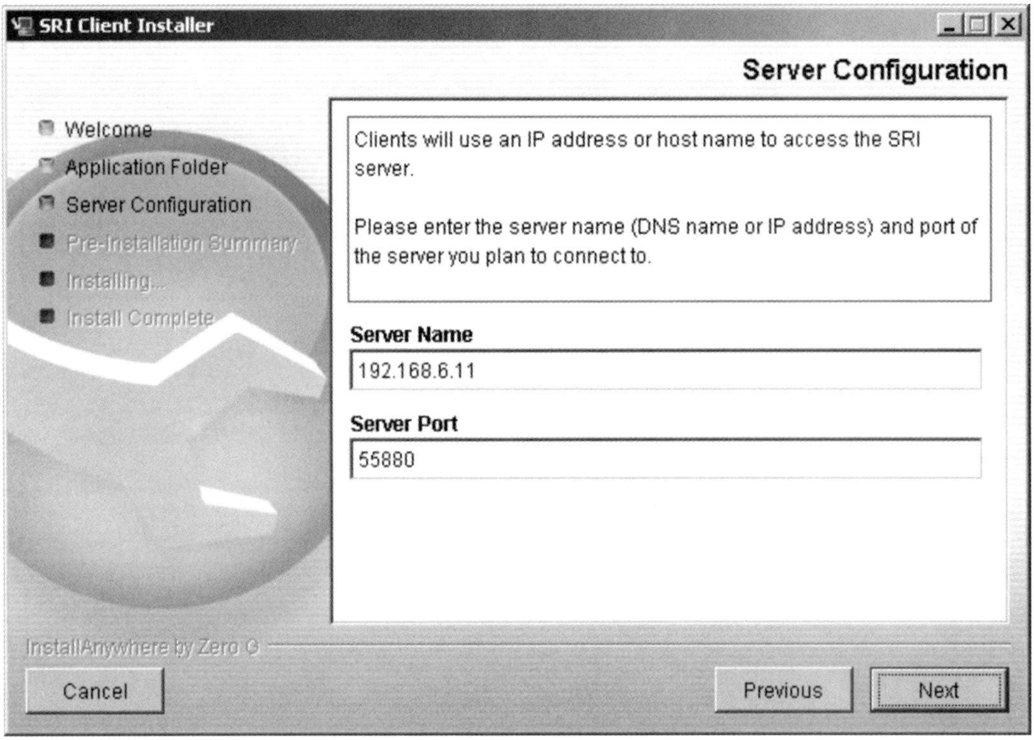

Note: The Server IP address and port number shown above are examples. Your IP address will be different; your port number may also be different.

Click **Next** to proceed.

5. Pre-Installation Summary

This screen displays the information about where ***SRI*** Enterprise Edition will be installed, as well as the resources needed to do so. It's important to review this screen carefully—particularly the space requirements—so you can be sure you have adequate space on the workstation for the installation.

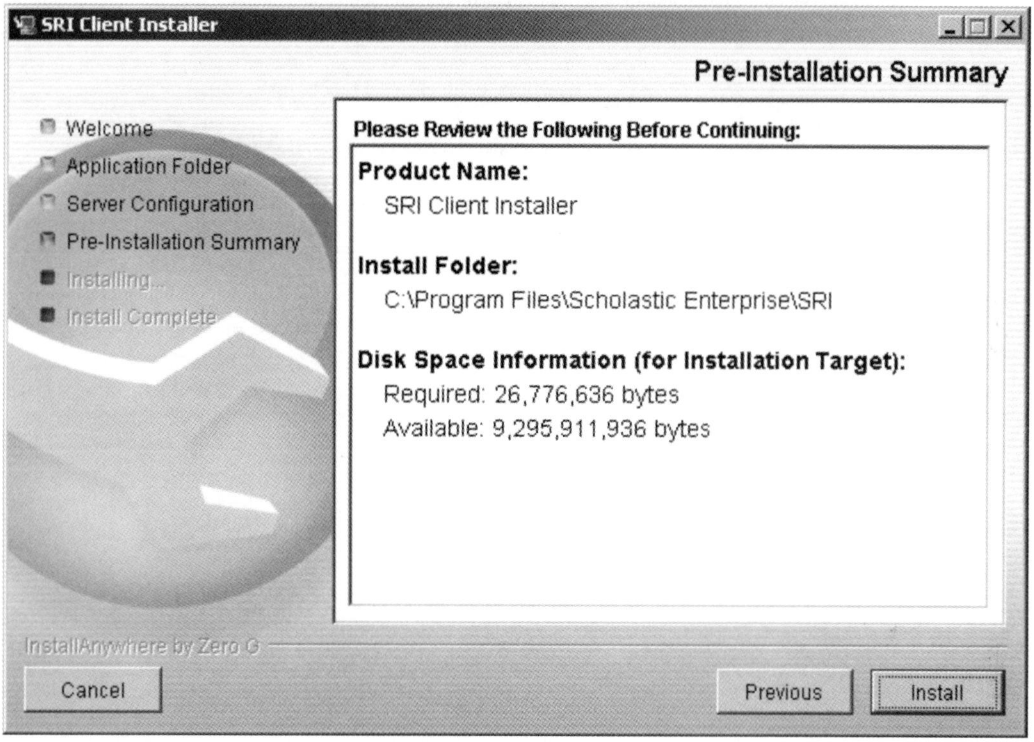

Click **Install** to proceed.

6. Install Complete

Once all the ***SRI Enterprise Edition*** Client files are installed, the **Install Complete** screen will display.

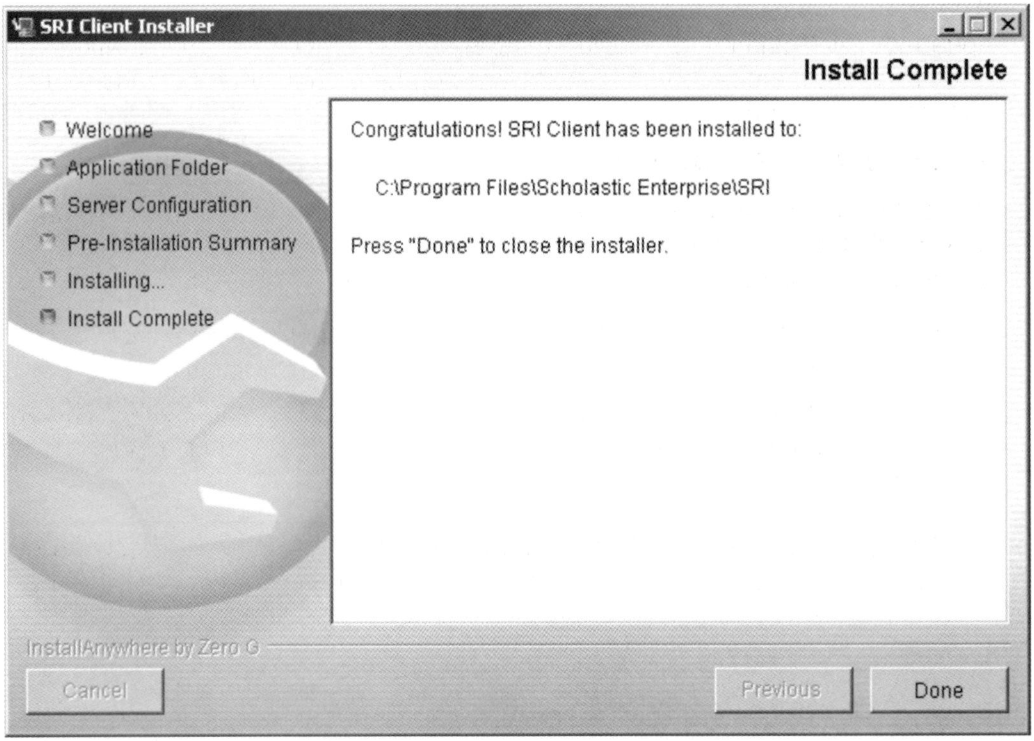

Click **Done** to end the ***SRI* Enterprise Edition** installation process.

The Installation window will close and the icon for SRI will be visible on your desktop.

Scholastic
Reading
Inventory

IMPORTANT NOTE ABOUT RIGHTS AND PERMISSIONS FOR CLIENT INSTALLATIONS

Limited-Access Users on all Installations:

If your Scholastic workstations have limited access permissions, you will need to update permissions after installing the Scholastic Client applications. Make sure that you grant them read/write permissions to the Scholastic Enterprise folder, including all files and subfolders.

Note for *SRI* on Mac OS X v10.4.x:

Due to the way permissions are handled on Mac OS X v10.4.x machines, an additional step is required. You will need to set permissions on the "hidden" folder named **Contents** under the ***SRI*** subfolder. To do this, follow these steps:

1. Using Finder, navigate to the ***SRI*** subfolder below the Scholastic Enterprise folder.
2. Control-click on the ***SRI*** executable inside that folder and select **Show Package Contents**. A new window will appear with the directory **Contents**.
3. Select the directory **Contents** and set the permissions to read/write for this folder and all subfolders for this user (and any other users that need access).

Activating Licenses

Once you have installed all of the Scholastic Suite programs, you must activate your licenses to make the programs accessible to students. To activate licenses:

1. Sign in to SAM and click the **My District** link at the top of the SmartBar to open the **My District Profile** screen.

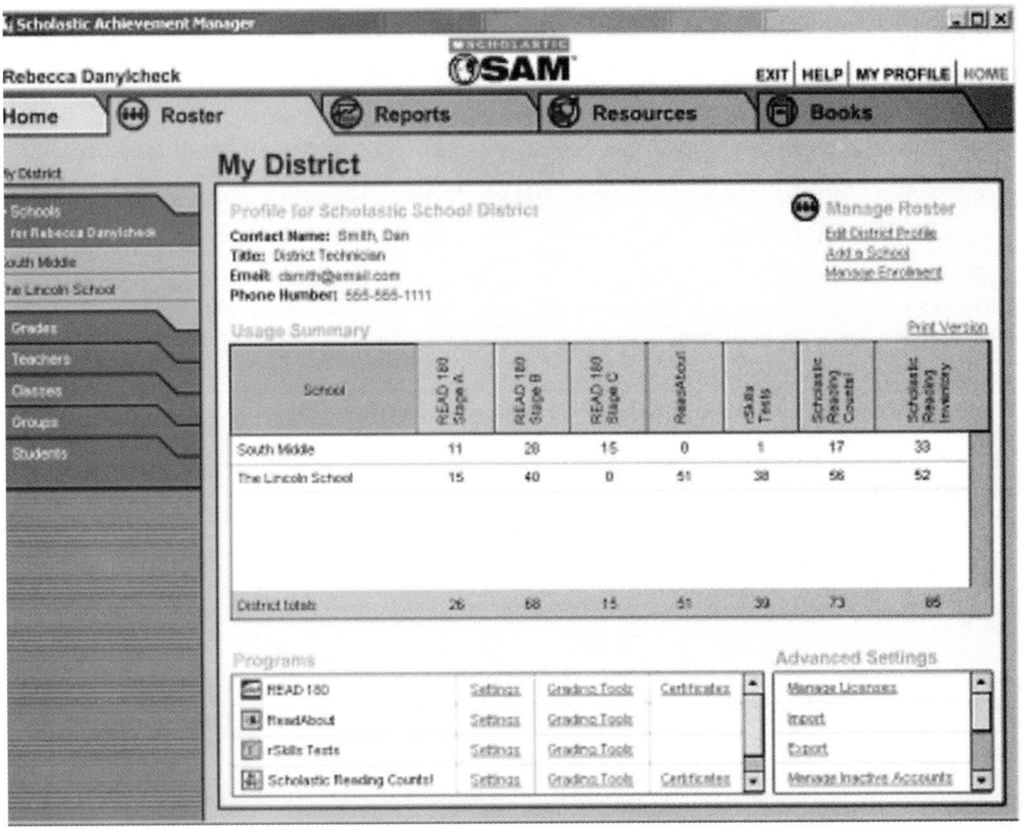

2. On the profile page, click **Manage Licenses** under **Advanced Settings** in the lower right of the screen. This will open the **Licensing** window and display the Installation Code.

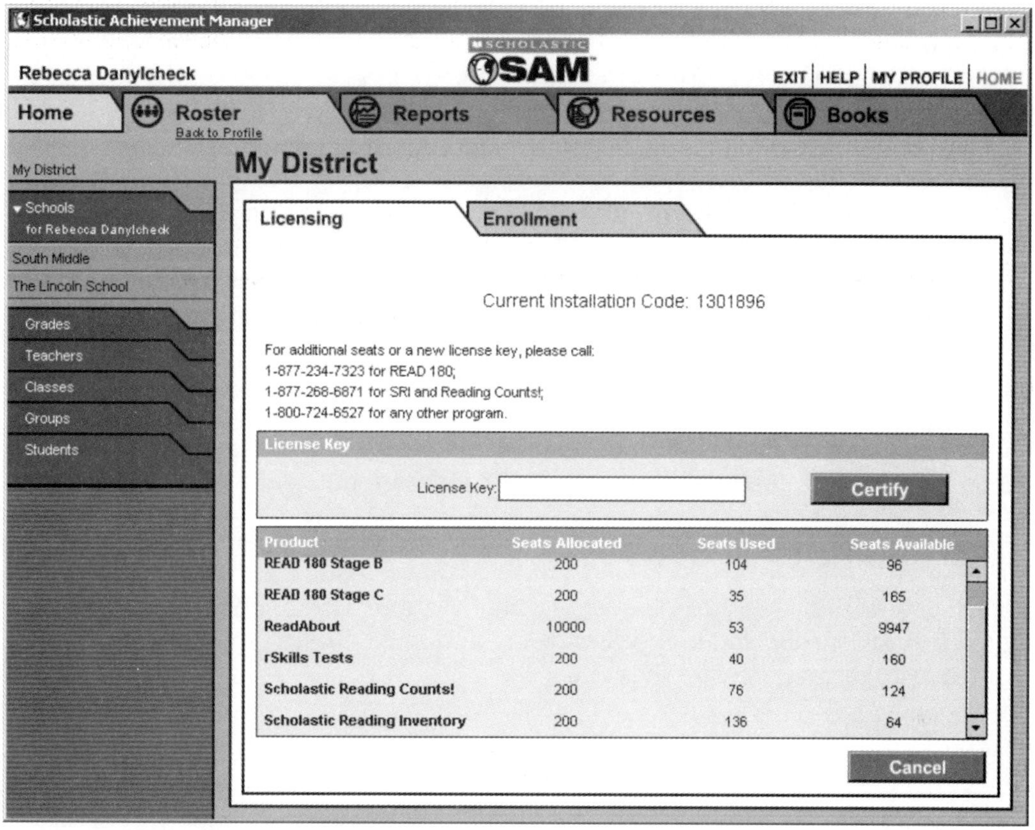

3. Once the information is displayed on the screen, call Scholastic Customer Service at 1-877-COUNTS1 (268-6871) between 7:00 A.M. and 6:00 P.M. CST, and provide the representative with your school or district address, zip code, and the installation code on the screen.

4. The representative will provide you with a License Key for each of the Scholastic programs you have bought. Enter the License Key and click the **Certify** button to activate the programs for the number of licenses your school or district has purchased.

SETTING UP AND MANAGING THE DATABASE

After installing all of the server software, installing the first SAM Client, and entering your license codes, you must set up the SAM database. This is done using the SAM Client. Certain basic steps are done manually. However, you also have the option to:

- Migrate data from an SMS installation.
- Import data from a different SAM installation.
- Import data from a non-Scholastic application (*.csv or *.xml files).

Important Note: If you plan to migrate data from an SMS system, you <u>must</u> do so before any teachers or students access SAM or any other Scholastic reading application. Once the first student uses any of the student programs, or a teacher signs in to SAM, the Data Migration feature is disabled. Instructions on Data Migration begin on page 81.

An Import of roster data can be performed at any time, regardless of who has accessed the SAM database. See **page 97** for more details.

SAM SmartBar Structure

Each user in SAM, as well as every District, School, Class, or Group, has a profile which is reflected in the SmartBar. You must create these profiles as part of the installation process. They are:

- District
- School
- Class
- Teacher
- Grade
- Student
- Group

NOTE: Every installation of SAM has an implied District account, whether you are using Scholastic programs in just one school or in several schools in a district. This District account provides a unified structure and gives compatibility between SAM installations. The District structure is what enables data aggregation, which is useful for broad-based reporting purposes. It also provides extensibility should you ever decide to add other schools to your SAM installation.

If a District is using multiple SAM servers (i.e., a SAM Server in each school), the District Name and State must be exactly the same on every SAM Server. If the District Names do not match, you will experience difficulties with Data Migration and Aggregation.

SAM Profile Creation

SAM profiles have a specific relationship and should be created in the following order:

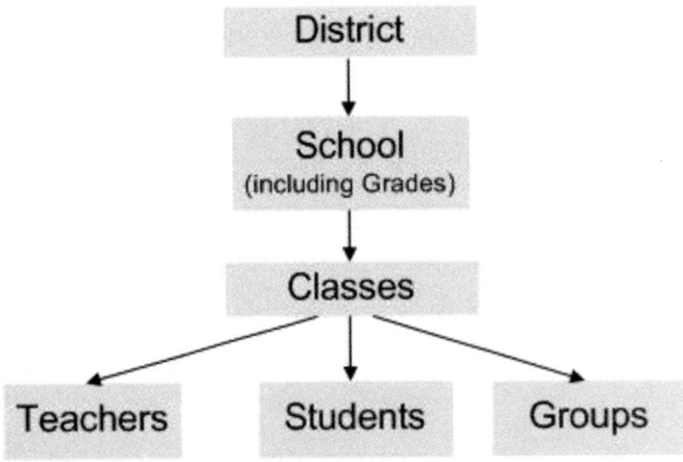

When you installed SAM, you automatically created a District. If you are not planning to populate the database by migrating data from an SMS installation, the next steps would be to create **School**, **Class**, **Teacher**, **Student**, and **Group** accounts, *in that order.*

Adding a School to SAM

Only District Administrators can add a school to SAM. The default school in SAM has the words "Enter Your School Name Here" in the School Name field. Be sure to double-click to select that school in the SmartBar and edit that school profile first before adding any additional schools.

To add a school:

1. Navigate to your **District Profile** window by clicking the **My District** link at the top of the SmartBar.

2. Click the **Add a School** link under **Manage Roster** in the upper right corner of your **My District Profile** screen. This opens the **Add a School** window.

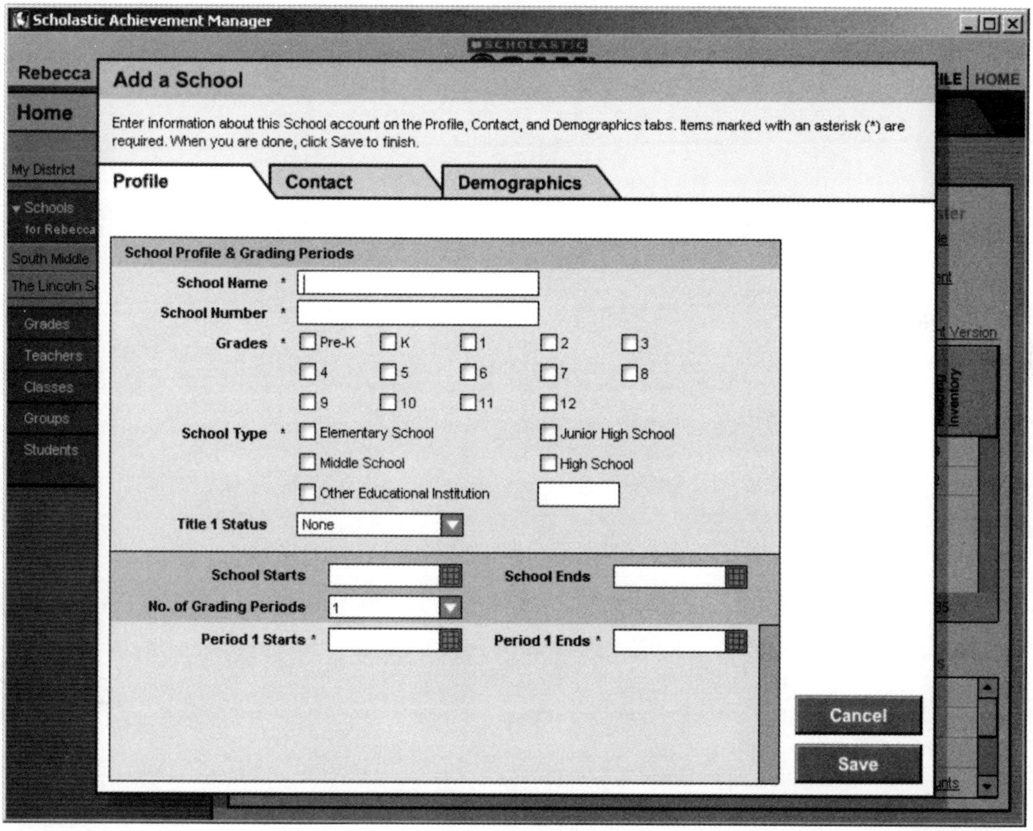

3. Enter the requested information. **(Information with an asterisk [*] is required.)**

    - Enter your **School Name** and **Number**.
    - Select the **Grades** that your school includes and the **School Type**.
    - If you have **Title 1** status, enter the appropriate selection. Otherwise, leave blank.
    - Enter the School **Start** and **End Date** and **Number of Grading Periods**. The default number of periods is one, however, you may enter up to six. If you choose more than one, you must enter the start and end date for each period. The final period end date must be the same as the School End date.
    - If you would like to add **Contact** or **Demographic** information, click on the appropriate tab at the top of the window.

4. Click **Save** to keep your changes and return to the **Profile** screen.

Adding a Class to SAM

Note: You must add **Classes** before creating profiles for **Teachers**, **Students**, or **Groups** in SAM.

1. Navigate to a **School Profile** window by double-clicking the **School Name** on the SmartBar and clicking the yellow **Roster** tab.

2. Click the **Add a Class** link under **Manage Roster** in the upper right corner of the **School Profile** screen. The **Add a Class** window will open.

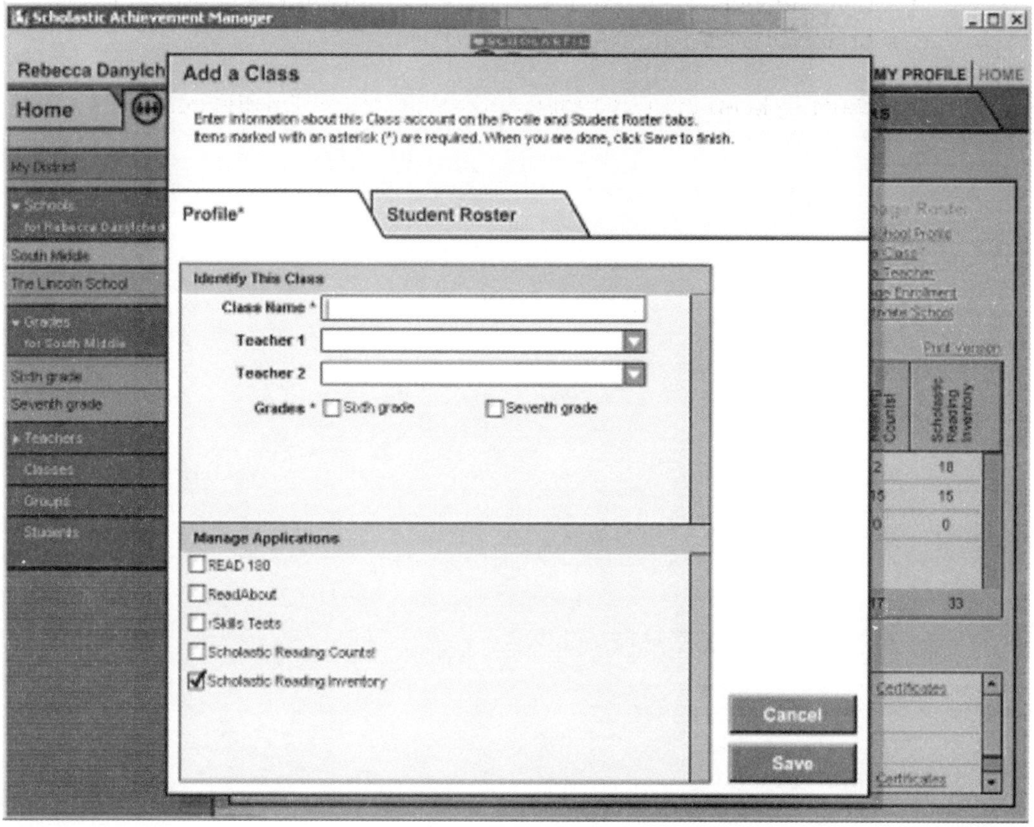

3. Enter the requested information. **(Information with an asterisk [*] is required.)**

    - Up to two teachers can be added to a class on this screen. More teachers can be added to the class in the **Edit Teacher** screen.
    - Classes do not need to be assigned to a teacher in this step. Teachers can be assigned to a class later.
    - If students are already in the database, they can be added to the class on the **Student Roster Screen**. Students can also be added to classes later.

4. Click **Save** to keep your changes and return to the **Profile** screen.

Adding a Teacher to SAM

Teachers must be assigned to one or more classes when they are added to SAM.

1. Navigate to a **School Profile** window by double-clicking the **School Name** on the SmartBar and clicking the yellow **Roster** tab.

2. Click the **Add a Teacher** link under **Manage Roster** in the upper right corner of the **School Profile** screen. The **Add a Teacher** window will open.

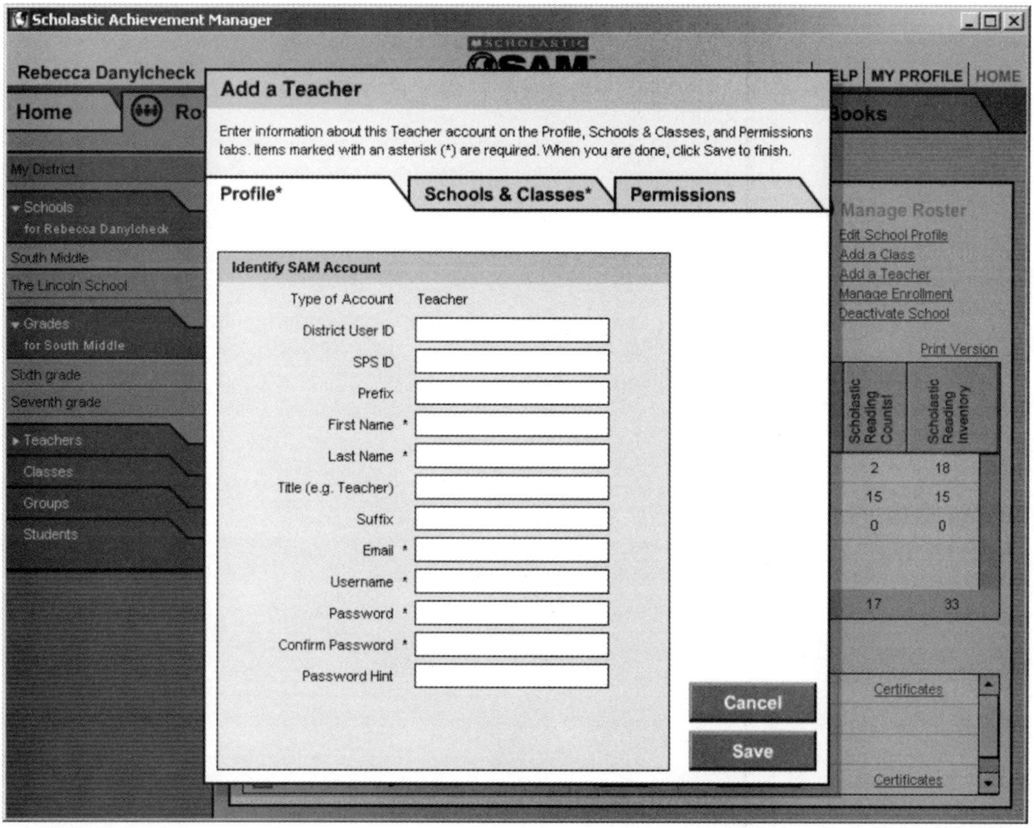

3. Enter the requested Profile information. **(Information with an asterisk [*] is required.)** This includes **First Name, Last Name**, **Email**, **Username**, **Password,** and **Confirm Password**. We also strongly recommend adding a **Password Hint**.

4. Click on the **Schools & Classes** tab. Check the boxes next to the classes that the teacher is associated with.

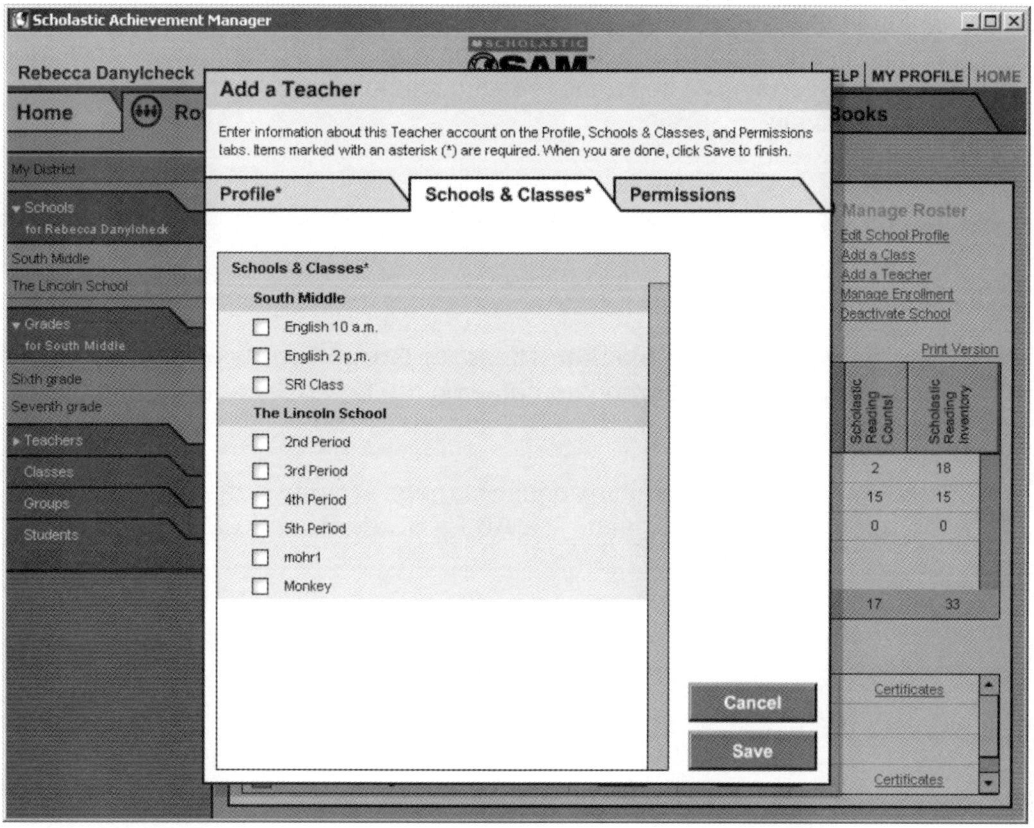

5. Click **Save** to keep your changes and return to the **Profile** screen.

Note: When you create a profile for a teacher, be sure you inform him or her of the Username and Password you created in his or her profile. Teachers may then change their passwords following instructions in the ***SRI Educator's Guide***.

Adding a Student to SAM

Though students will not use the SAM Client software, each student is represented in the database by a profile. You may add students to the database by creating a profile in SAM or by migrating or importing student data. For more information on migrating or importing, see the sections that begin on **pages 81** and **97**, respectively.

Students must be assigned to one or more classes when they are added to SAM.

Creating an individual student profile:

1. Navigate to a **Grade**, **Teacher**, **Class**, or **Group Profile** window by double-clicking the appropriate name on the SmartBar and clicking the yellow **Roster** tab.

2. Click the **Add a Student** link under **Manage Roster** in the upper right corner of the **Profile** screen. The **Add a Student** window will open.

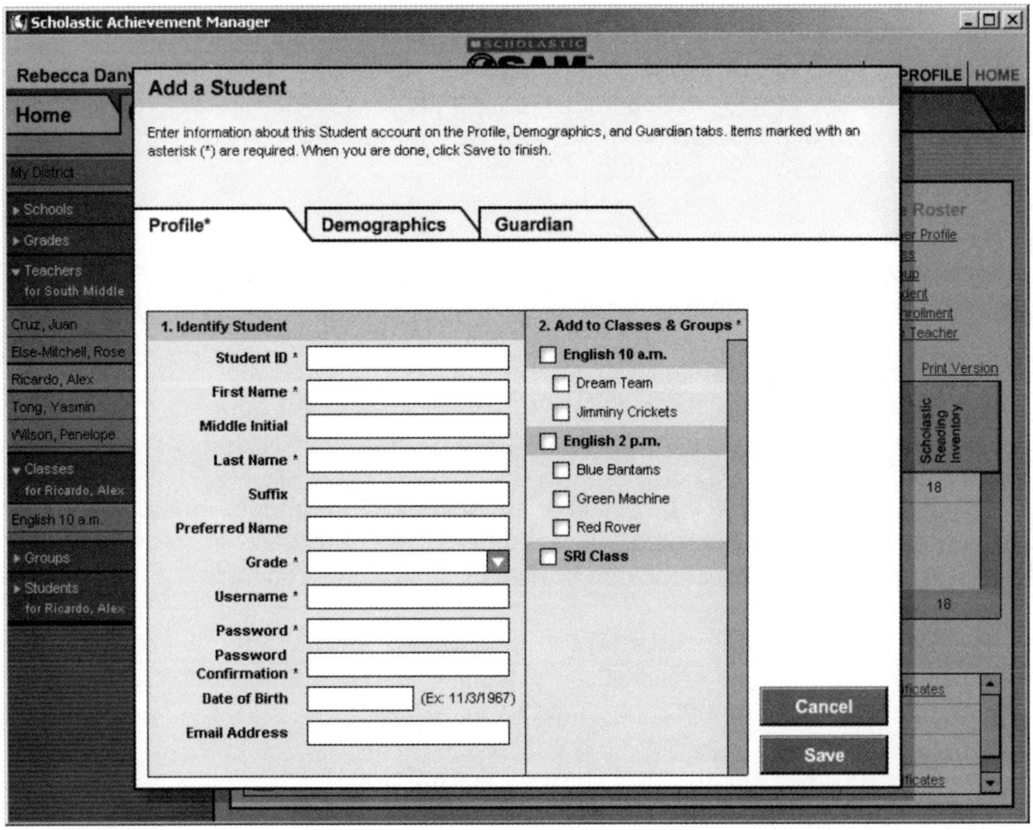

3. Enter the requested information. **(Information with an asterisk [*] is required.)**

4. Click **Save** to keep your changes and return to the **Profile** screen.

User Accounts and Permissions

For security purposes, SAM uses permissions to allow different levels of access to student information, settings, and performance data. Permissions are based on the type of account that is created for each user.

User Account Types

There are four account types in SAM. Each school may choose different levels of access based on the technical setup.

The four account types are:

- **Teachers:** These accounts are for classroom-based educators, including teachers, teaching assistants, and reading coaches.

- **School Administrators:** These accounts have management or administrative responsibilities for multiple educators within a single school. These could include principals or reading coaches.

- **District Administrators:** These accounts have management or administrative responsibilities for multiple school administrators, and subsequently for a number of different schools.

- **School Technicians and District Technicians:** These accounts are for the primary technical contacts for the school or district systems using Scholastic programs. Technical coordinators may be responsible for one school or several schools.

Account type and permissions are assigned during the setup process, but may be changed by an administrator at any time to suit your or your particular school's needs. For example, you may be a teacher as well as the technical administrator in a building and need to have access to the administrative functions of SAM.

Default Settings for Permissions

Users with Administrative accounts may change all permissions settings.

	Teacher		School Administrator		District Administrator		School Technician		District Technician	
Component	View	Edit	View	Edit	View	Edit	View	Edit	View	Edit
Own profile (My Profile)	√	√	√	√	√	√	√	√	√	√
Permissions (Own)	√	N/A	√	N/A	√	N/A	√	N/A	√	N/A
Edit Student	√	√	√	√	√	√	√	√	√	√
Edit Group	√	√	√	√	√	√	√	√	√	√
Edit Class	√	√	√	√	√	√	√	√	√	√
Edit Teacher	X !	X !	√	√	√	√	√	√	√	√
Edit School	X !	X !	√	√	√	√	√	√	√	√
Edit District	X !	X !	X !	X !	√	√	X !	X !	√	√
Permissions (Others)	X !	X !	√	√	√	√	√	√	√	√
Manage All Accounts (Manage Inactive Accounts)	X		√		√		√		√	
Add Students	√		√		√		√		√	
Add Groups	√		√		√		√		√	
Add Classes	√		√		√		√		√	
Add Teachers	X		√		√		√		√	
Add Schools	X !		X !		√		X !		√	

LEGEND:

√	Offered at default.
X	Privilege not offered at default.
!	User cannot access page/link/button, even if permission were granted.
N/A	Permission does not exist.

Default Settings for Permissions, Continued

Component	Teacher	School Administrator	District Administrator	School Technician	District Technician
Deactivate Student	X	√	√	√	√
Deactivate Group	√	√	√	√	√
Deactivate Class	X	√	√	√	√
Deactivate Teacher	X !	√	√	√	√
Deactivate School	X !	X	√	X	√
Import Data	X	√	√	√	√
View Demographics (Edit Student Popup)	√	√	√	√	√
Export Data	X	√	√	√	√
Manage Student Application Settings	√	√	√	√	√
NCLB Filter (Demographic Filter on each report)	√	√	√	√	√
Subgroup Setup (Demographic tab on District/School Profile pages)	X !	√	√	√	√
License Key Input	X !	√	√	√	√

LEGEND:

√	Offered at default.
X	Privilege not offered at default.
!	User cannot access page/link/button, even if permission were granted.
N/A	Permission does not exist.

Note: District Administrators can change permissions for any other administrator or teacher. School Administrators can change permissions for any other administrator or teacher within their school.

Changing Permissions

As a School or District Technician, you can change permissions to allow access to different parts of SAM. You can do this in the **Edit Profile** window, which you can access from any **Profile** screen.

To change permissions in SAM:

1. To change a Teacher's permissions: double-click the **SmartBar** to select a teacher, and click the **Edit Teacher Profile** link under **Manage Roster** on the top right part of the screen.

   To change an Administrator's permissions: choose **Manage Administrative Accounts** from **Advanced Settings** on the lower right of an Administrator's profile screen, then select the administrative account for which you would like to change permissions.

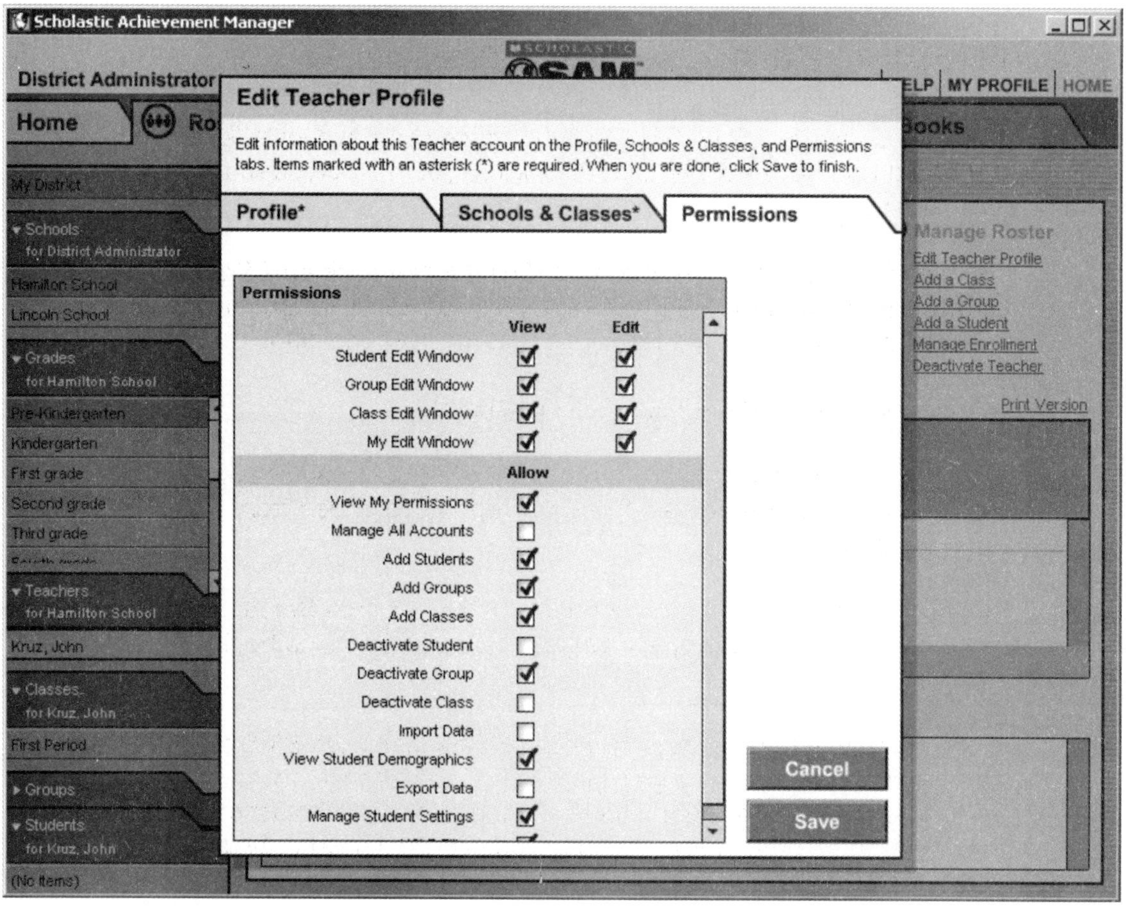

2. Click the **Permissions** tab to view the current permissions settings.

3. Check the boxes to select (or deselect) the desired permissions.

4. Click **Save** when you are done to save the new settings and return to the **Profile** screen. Click **Cancel** to return to the **Profile** screen without saving your changes.

Uninstalling Existing Scholastic Programs

If you are converting from SMS to SAM, once you have installed SAM Server and Client and have verified that they work, you may proceed with uninstalling SMS and your previous ***SRI*** program.

You may find it useful to refer to your ***SRI 3.x Network and Stand-Alone Installation Guide***, to reference the folder structures in Appendix B. This will help you verify that you are removing only the files that should be removed.

To uninstall SMS and previous ***SRI*** installations:

1. Perform a standard backup of your SMS database, saving the backup onto off-system media. Print any reports you need from the SMS database.

2. If you have not already done so, install the SAM Server and SAM Client and ensure that they are working. (See instructions beginning on **page 17**.)

3. If you want, you may migrate your database from SMS to SAM. See instructions beginning on **page 81**. If you choose not to migrate data, you must use a different method to bring existing Scholastic data into SAM (i.e., add it manually or import *.csv or *.xml files) or begin with a new database.

4. Verify that data exists on SAM after migration by signing in to SAM and reviewing data.

5. Uninstall previous Scholastic software (SRI 3.0x; SMS) from all student workstations. Follow instructions in the ***SRI 3.x Network and Stand-Alone Installation Guide*** for uninstalling the ***SRI*** Workstations. For more information, see Appendix G on **page 171**, which addresses uninstallation issues.

6. Using the Windows Explorer (or Apple Finder) locate the **SCHSUITE** folder on your server.

7. Verify that nothing other than ***SRI*** and SMS database folders exist in this folder (i.e., ensure that you have not installed SAM into this folder). You may review Appendix B in the ***SRI 3.x Network and Stand-Alone Installation Guide*** to verify what should be in this folder. Once you are sure that only the previous Scholastic programs and data exist in the **SCHSUITE** folder, delete it.

DATA MOVEMENT

This section covers the several different types of functions that you can use to import and export roster and performance data. You can:

- migrate data from SMS into SAM.
- import roster and performance data from non-SAM applications.
- export roster and performance data for use in non-SAM applications.
- aggregate SAM data on a centralized server.
- back up data.

For details on exactly what data can be imported or exported by each function refer to Appendix C1 on **page 161**.

MIGRATING DATA FROM THE SMS

If you have replaced a Scholastic Management System (SMS) installation with a SAM installation, you may move the data from the old system to the new one using a process called Data Migration.

This is a four-step process which requires access to both SMS and SAM. All steps of the process must be performed by a SAM user with administrative permissions. You may only migrate data from an SMS v1.6 installation.

Important Note: Migration is only possible when the legacy SMS installation and the new SAM installation have the exact same Scholastic programs, i.e., if SMS has **SRI** and **SRC**, the SAM installation must also have **SRI** and **SRC** Enterprise Editions.

If you are using v1.5, contact Scholastic Technical Support at 1-800-283-5974 so you can upgrade to v1.6 and migrate your data.

The data migration steps are:

1. The SMS data must be prepared using the **SMS Data Prep Tool**, which will produce two files for migration into SAM: student performance data (*.smx) and SRC! quiz data (*.zip), if you are migrating SRC! data to SAM.

2. The second step is to install the SRC quiz data (*.zip) into the SAM installation using the **SRC! Quiz Manager**.

3. The student performance data (*.smx) can then be migrated into SAM using the **SMS Data Migration Tool**.

4. Finally, the newly migrated student accounts must be activated in SAM from the **Managing Inactive Accounts** link in SAM.

Important Note: You may only migrate data from a SMS v1.6 or an SRI/SRC 3.0x installation. If you are running an earlier version of the SMS and related programs, you must upgrade your SMS installation before you can migrate data into a new SAM installation.

The data migration tools for SMS and SAM are on the **SAM Server Installation Disc 1.**

Step 1: SMS Data Preparation

The **SMS Data Preparation Tool** is a separate utility application designed to look into an SMS database and prepare two output files for migration into SAM.

To prepare SMS data:

1. Launch the **SMS Data Preparation Tool** (PC or Mac) from the SAM Server Installation Disc 1.

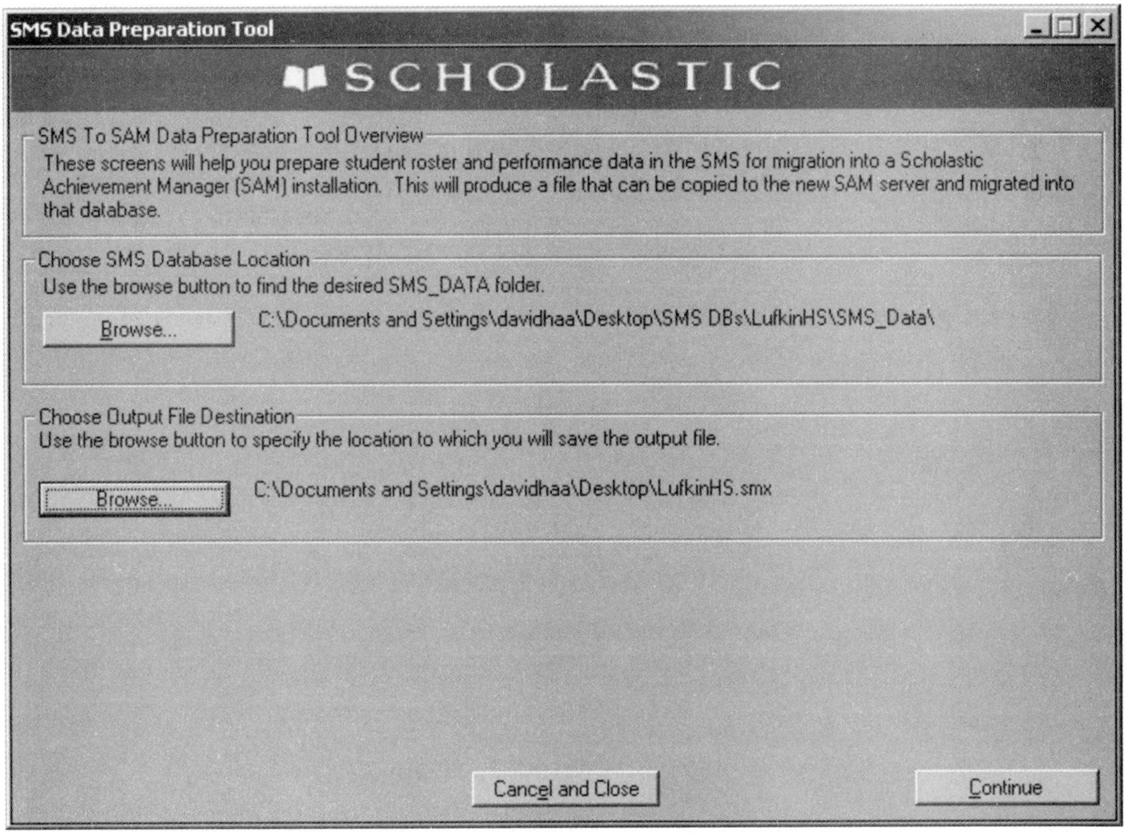

There are two **Browse** buttons on the first screen. Using the first **Browse** button, locate the SMS_DATA directory from the desired SMS installation. Using the second **Browse** button, select the location where you wish to place the output files and click **Continue**.

You may want to begin the process by creating a folder on your desktop named SMS Migrations, which you can then select as the **Output File Destination**.

If you are doing multiple migrations, be sure to give each file a name that reflects its contents.

2. A roster of students in the selected SMS database will appear. Click the boxes to select individual students' accounts for migration. You can select or deselect all students using the buttons at the bottom of the screen and click **Continue**.

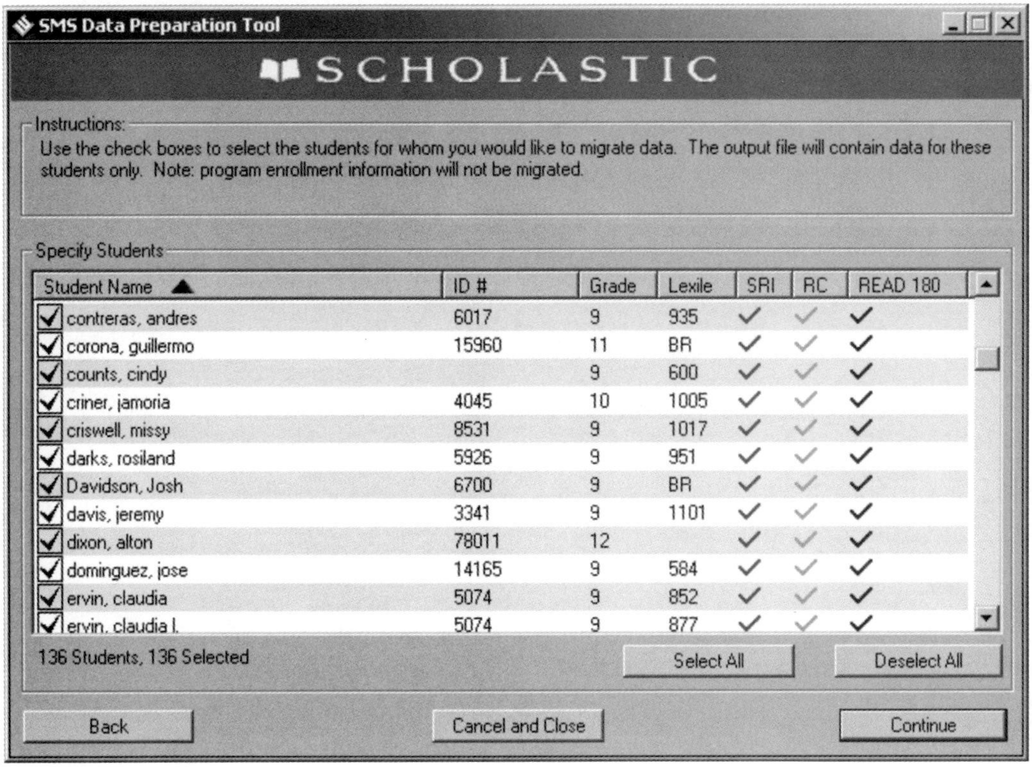

3. A **Summary** screen will appear so that you can review all of the selections you have made before processing the data. Click the **Back** button to return to previous screens and make changes. When you are ready to proceed, click **Prepare Data**.

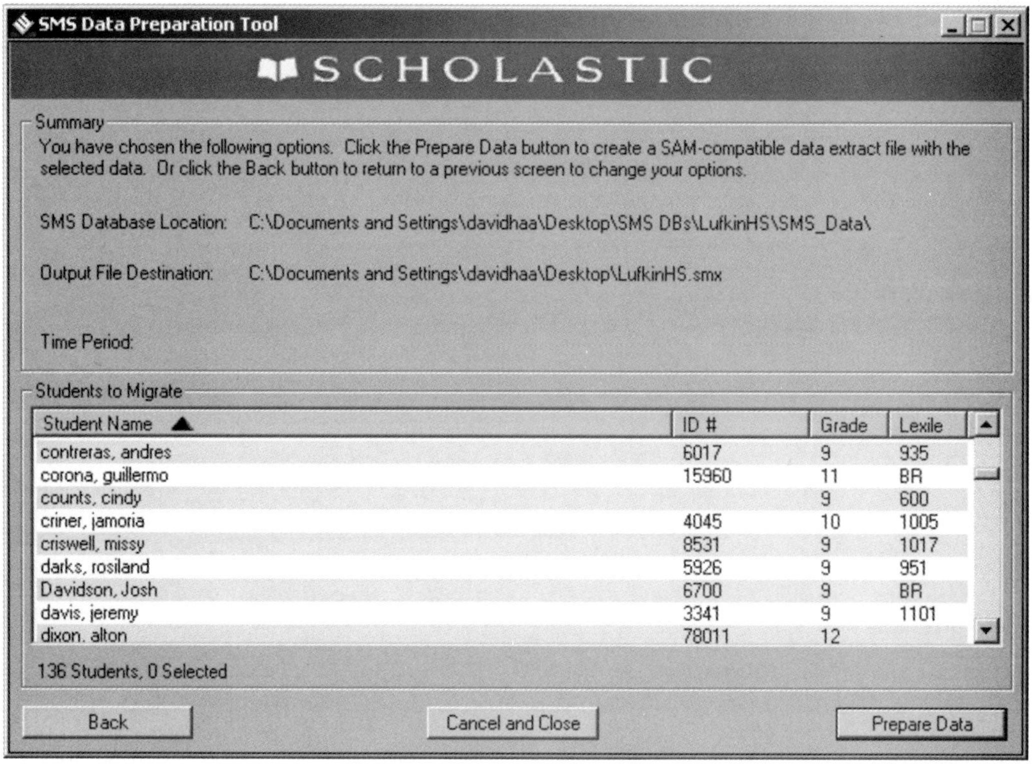

4. Processing the SMS data may take several minutes, and a progress bar will indicate the level of completion. When the process is finished, a completion screen will display the details of the process.

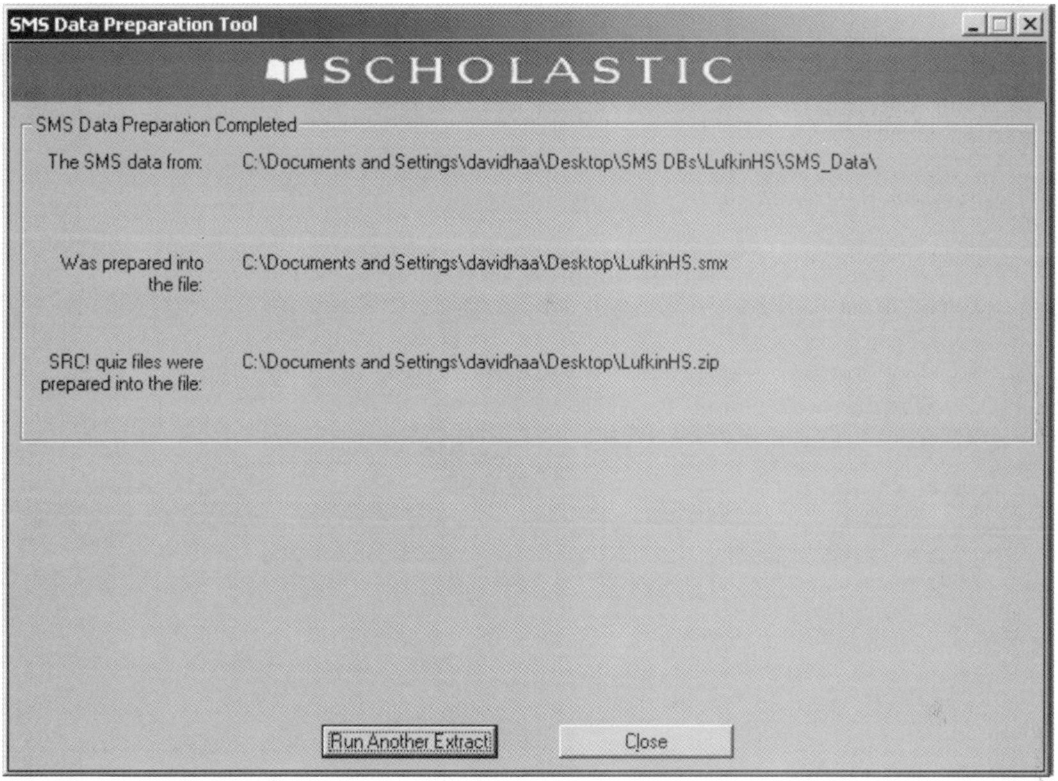

You may now choose to close the **SMS Data Preparation Tool** or click **Run Another Extract** to prepare data from a different SMS database.

Step 2: Scholastic Reading Counts! Quiz Installation

If you were running **SRC!** on the SMS installation, you will need to install quizzes onto SAM for your new **SRC!** installation.

After preparing the data from the SMS installation in Step 1 above, copy the .smx and .zip files to your SAM server, if they are not already on the destination SAM server.

To install Scholastic Reading Counts! quizzes:

1. Double-click the SAM icon on the desktop and sign in to SAM.
2. Click the **Books** tab to open the **Scholastic Reading Counts! Book Expert**.
3. Click the **Scholastic Reading Counts! Quiz Manager** tab. The **Quiz Manager** will display.

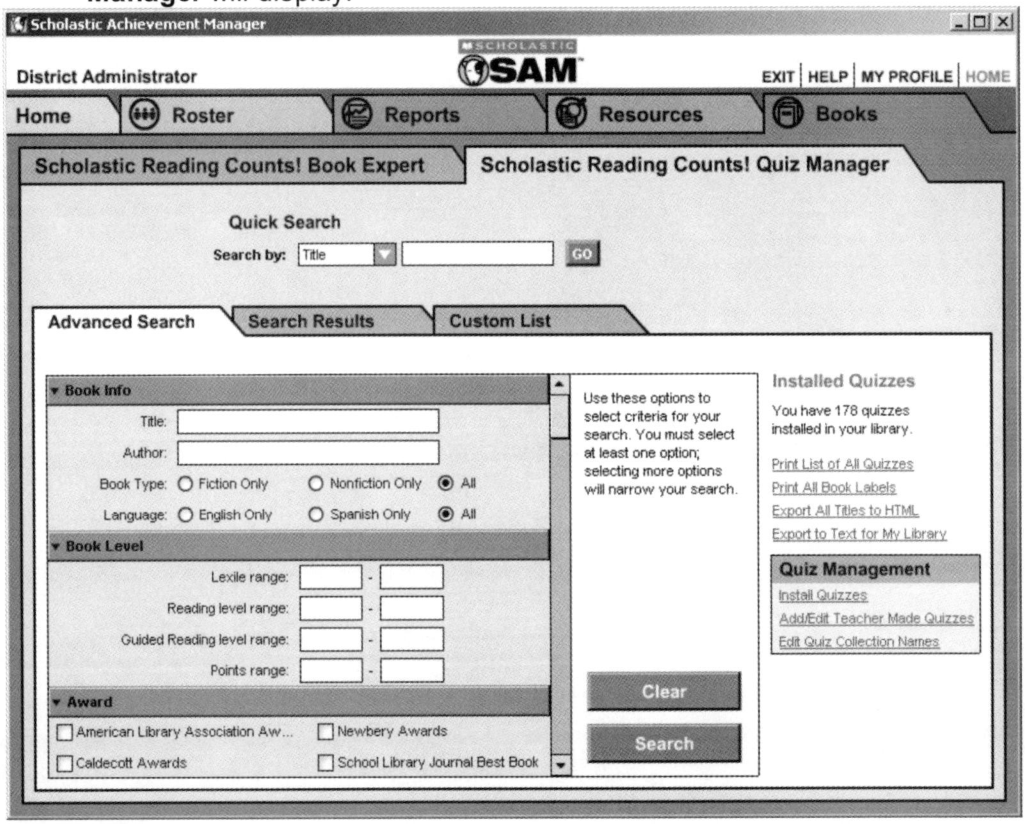

4. Click the **Install Quizzes** link under **Quiz Management**, on the lower right of the screen. The **Install Quizzes Wizard** will open in a separate window.

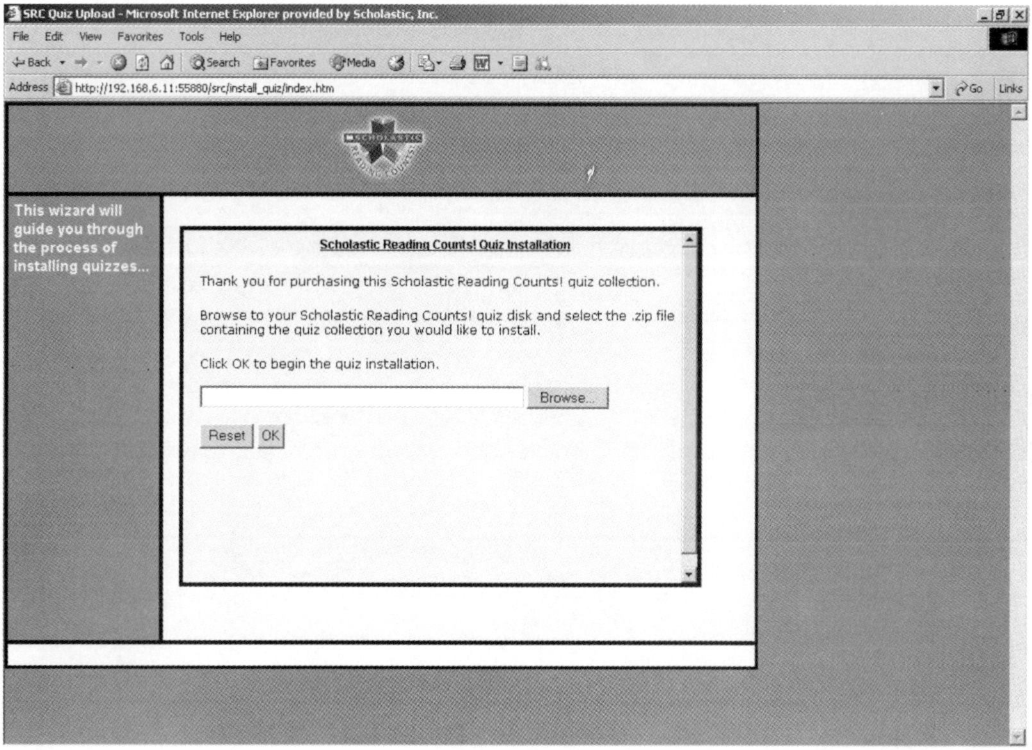

5. Click the **Browse** button; a **Choose File** window will open.

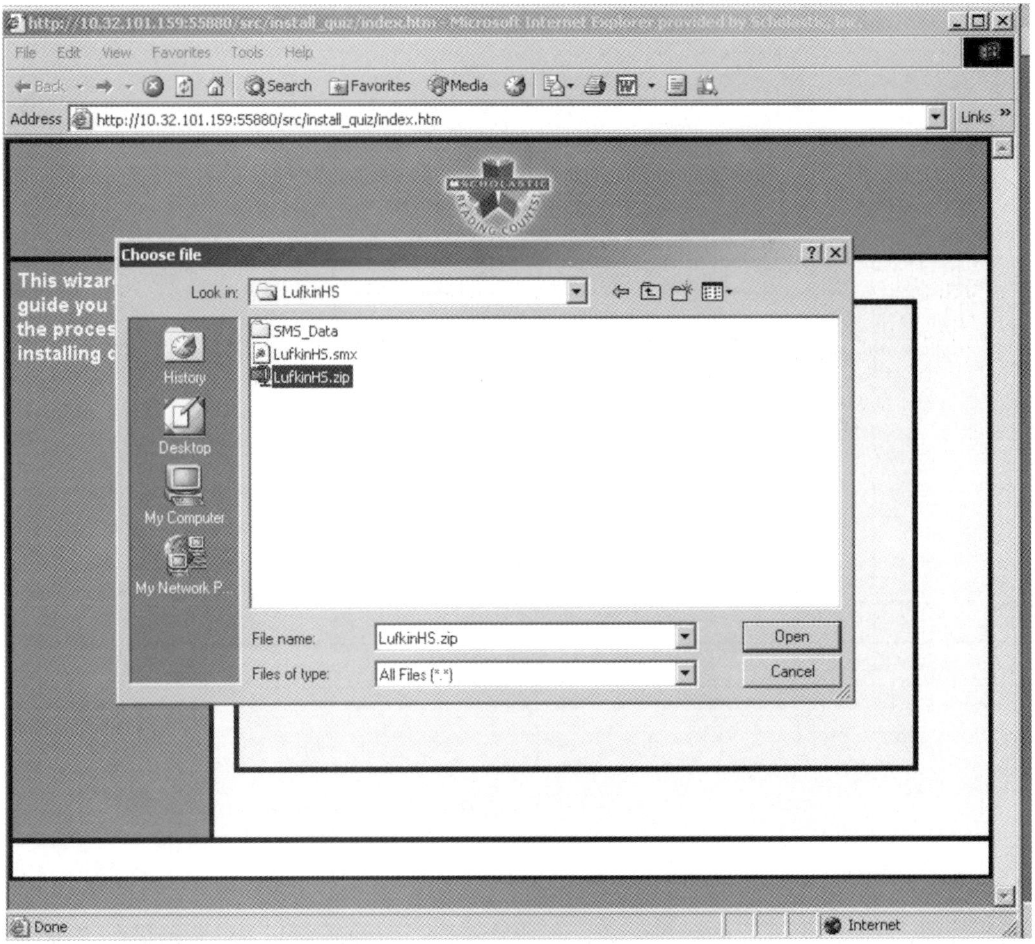

Use the **Look in** pull-down menu to navigate to the .zip file that was created in the **SMS Data Preparation Tool** and click **Open**. The **File Upload** window will close, returning you to the **Install Quizzes Wizard**.

6. Click **OK** to begin quiz installation. Once the quizzes have installed, you will see a success screen.

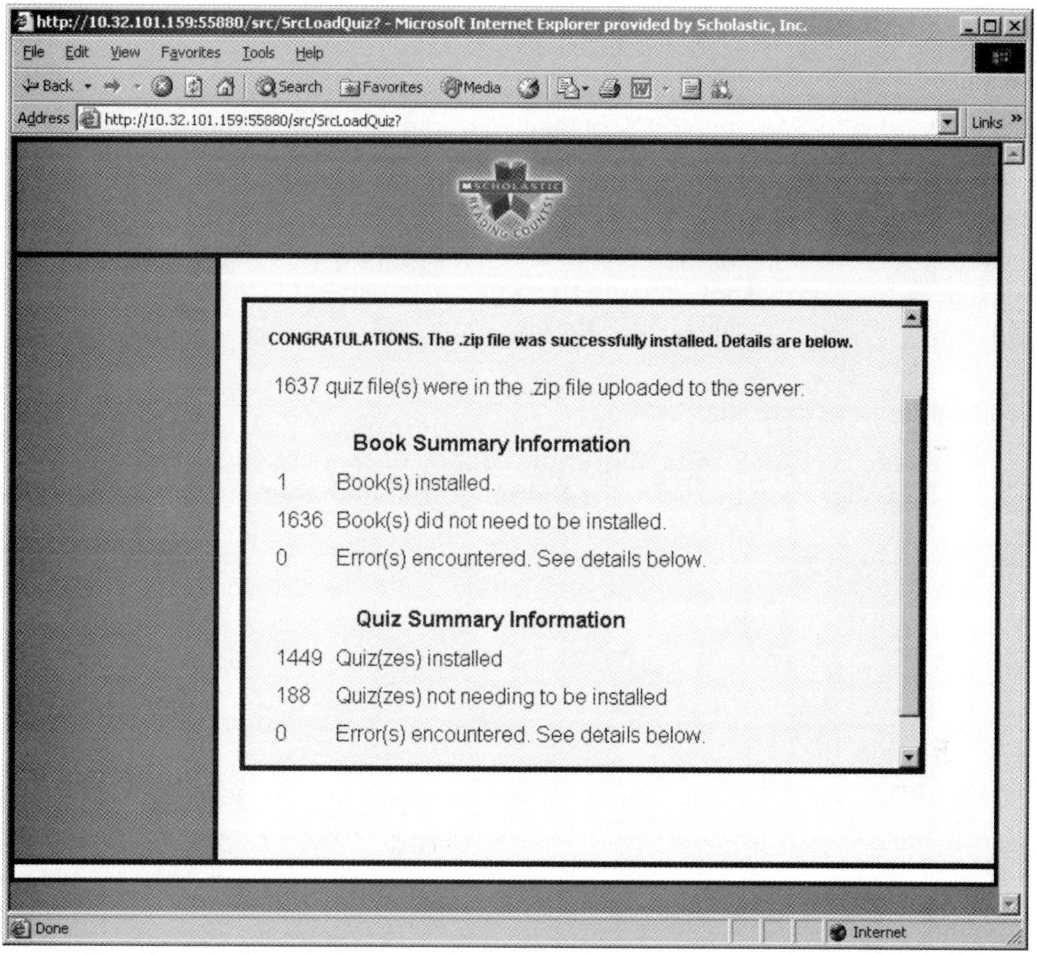

7. Close the browser window to return to SAM. You will now be able to access all the quizzes installed in SAM.

Step 3: SMS Data Migration

Once you have installed the Scholastic Reading Counts! quizzes that were migrated from the SMS, you may migrate all of your student rosters into SAM.

> **Note:** This step ***cannot*** be performed if a student or teacher has signed in to SAM or used Scholastic programs on the new installation. Once someone has signed on to the new system, data can no longer be migrated from the SMS.

Data migration is done in a special application separate from SAM called the **SMS Data Migration Tool**. You will need to have your SAM server IP address (**page 29**) available to utilize the Data Migration Tool.

To migrate SMS data into SAM:

1. Launch the **SMS Data Migration Tool** by double-clicking on the **SMSMigration.bat** file in the **SMSMigrationManager\bin** directory.

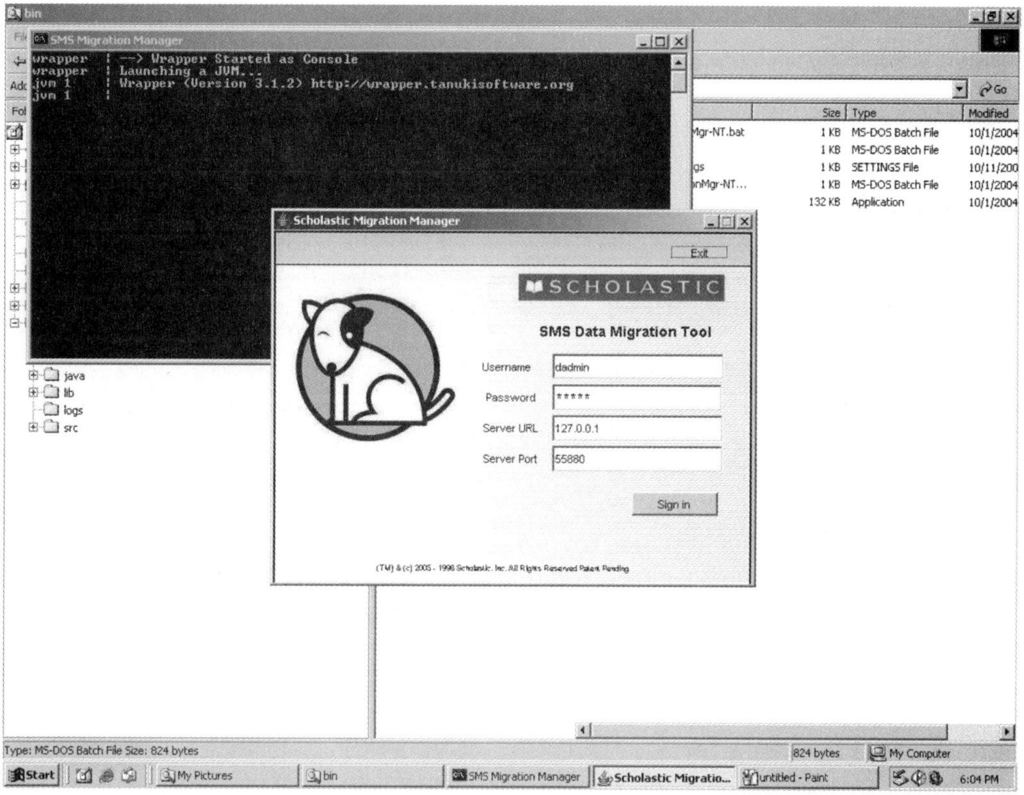

The sign-in screen will open.

2. Enter the Administrator **username**, **password**, **IP address**, and **port number** of the SAM server into which you want to migrate the SMS data and click **Sign in**.

3. Use the **Browse** button to locate the student performance data (*.smx) prepared by the **SMS Data Preparation Tool**. Or, type in the pathname in the edit box on-screen and click **Next**. A confirmation screen will display.

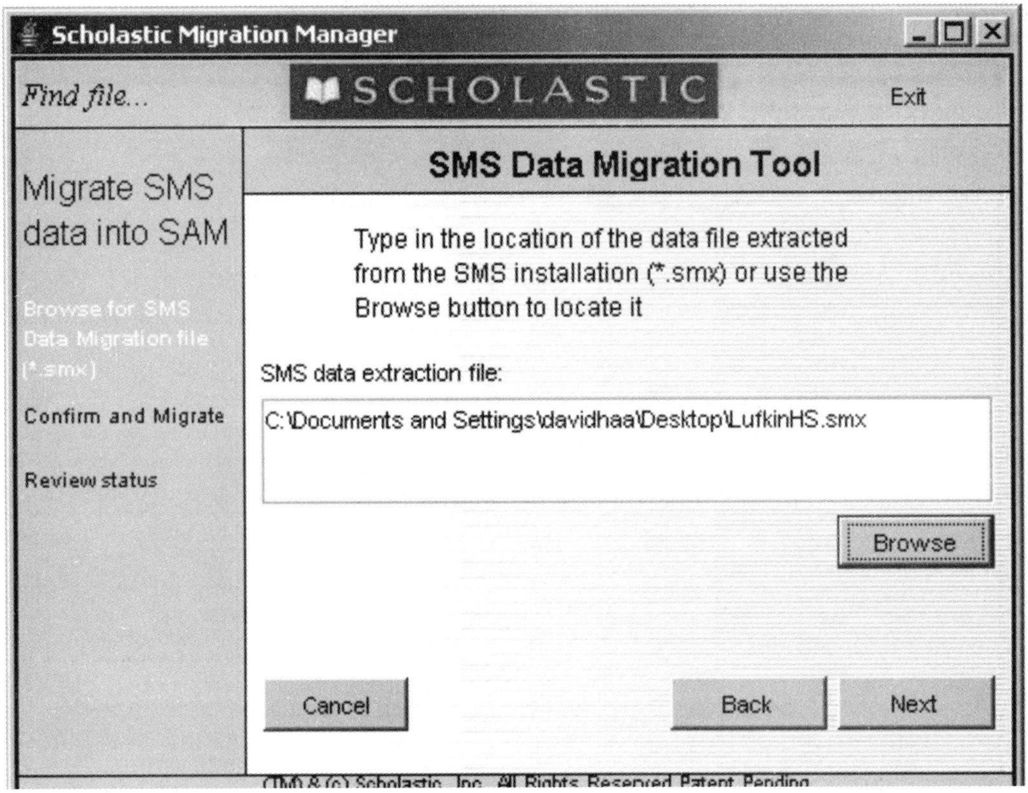

4. Once you have reviewed the filename then click **Next**.

5. A confirmation screen will appear. Review the information carefully (migration is irreversible) and then click **Migrate** when you are ready to begin the process.

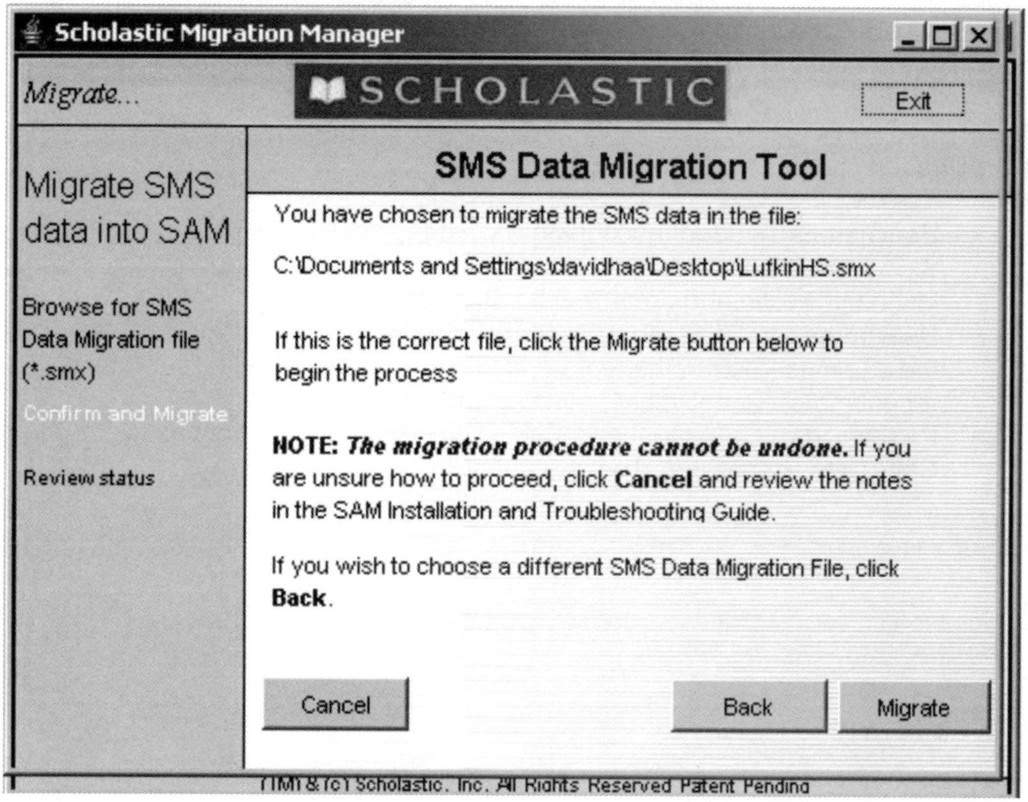

Once the process is complete, the final screen will display the status of the migration into SAM and the application can be closed.

If data from other SMS databases have been prepared, you may also click **Run New Migration** to migrate additional data.

6. Details of the migrated data will be sent in a log file to your Message Center on your SAM Home Page. The log file can also be found on the SAM server in the following directory: <root-drive>**\ScholasticEE\SAM_Server\jboss\server\lycea\log\migration**

Step 4: Activating Migrated Accounts

Once student data has been migrated, each migrated student account will appear in **Manage Inactive Accounts**. Each **student must be assigned to a class** and **enrolled** in the appropriate Scholastic programs. See **page 103** for specific instructions on using the **Manage Inactive Accounts** function in SAM.

Note: The following modifications to SMS student account data might appear in the migration process from SMS to SAM:

- **Usernames:** Student account in SMS does not have a username, so the SMS Data Preparation Tool creates one by joining the student's first and last names together: John Smith = JohnSmith.
- **Usernames in SAM must be unique:** If the SMS Migration Tool detects the same username, the tool will add a sequential number to the most recent match; JohnSmith1, JohnSmith2, etc.
- **Passwords:** If a student account in SMS does not have a password, the SMS Data Preparation Tool will supply the word, **password**.

IMPORTING AND EXPORTING

Importing Roster Data

Several different types of data can be imported into SAM. Because importing data will modify your database, it is important to do a database backup before proceeding with any file import. Only SAM users with administrative permissions may perform these functions.

SAM supports the import of **.csv, .xml,** and **.zip** files.
SAM will not import **.txt** files or **.xls** files.

You can import data for several different purposes:

1. For files from a different SAM installation (*.zip extension):
   - Create an **aggregated database** by combining data from several different SAM installations in your district into one larger database. This will facilitate running district-wide reports.
   - **Transfer** students from a different school into your SAM installation.
   - **Import SRI scores** for students in your SAM installation.

   Note: Do ***not*** unzip .zip files to be imported; SAM does this as part of the import process.

2. For non-SAM files (*.xml or *.csv extension):
   - **Import student roster** data from non-SAM programs into your SAM installation (using a .csv or .xml file format).

Note: All the records in an *.xml or *.csv file for import must have all required fields filled in or the import will fail. These required fields are:

- SIS_ID
- FIRST_NAME
- LAST_NAME
- USERNAME
- GRADE

Other fields may be left blank, but keep in mind the following:

- If nothing is entered for PASSWORD, the default will be **password**.
- If a duplicate USERNAME exists, SAM will add digits sequentially to render it unique.
- If an optional field is blank and data exists for that record, the existing data will remain; blank fields will not overwrite.

The following table details what fields can be imported into SAM in a *.xml or *.csv file:

Descriptive SAM Reference	Column Head (field name)	Data Type	Allowable Special Characters
Student ID	SIS_ID	[alpha-numeric]	—
First Name	FIRST_NAME	[alpha-numeric]	—
Middle Initial	MIDDLE_NAME	[alpha-numeric]	—
Last Name	LAST_NAME	[alpha-numeric]	—
Username	USER_NAME	[alpha-numeric]	[apostrophe], [hyphen], [space], [underscore]
Password	PASSWORD	[alpha-numeric]	[apostrophe], [hyphen], [space], [underscore]
Grade	GRADE	[Numeric]	—
Gender: Male	GENDER_MALE	[Y/N], [y/n]	—
Gender: Female	GENDER_FEMALE	[Y/N], [y/n]	—
School	SCHOOL_NAME	[alpha-numeric]	—
Class	CLASS_NAME	[alpha-numeric]	—
Ethnicity: White/Caucasian	ETHNIC_CAUCASIAN	[Y/N], [y/n]	—
Ethnicity: Black/African American	ETHNIC_AFRICAN_AM	[Y/N], [y/n]	—
Ethnicity: Hispanic	ETHNIC_HISPANIC	[Y/N], [y/n]	—
Ethnicity: Pacific Islander	ETHNIC_PACIFIC_ISL	[Y/N], [y/n]	—
Ethnicity: American Indian/Alaskan Native	ETHNIC_AM_IND_AK_NATIVE	[Y/N], [y/n]	—
Ethnicity: Asian	ETHNIC_ASIAN	[Y/N], [y/n]	—
AYP: Economically Disadvantaged	AYP_ECON_DISADVANTAGED	[Y/N], [y/n]	—
AYP: Limited English Proficiency	AYP_LTD_ENGLISH_PROFICIENCY	[Y/N], [y/n]	—
AYP: Gifted and Talented	AYP_GIFTED_TALENTED	[Y/N], [y/n]	—
AYP: Migrant	AYP_MIGRANT	[Y/N], [y/n]	—
AYP: Students with Disabilities	AYP_WITH_DISABILITIES	[Y/N], [y/n]	—

See Appendix C2 beginning on **page 162** for templates for *.xml and *.csv files to be imported into SAM.

To import data:

1. Double-click **My District** at the top of the SmartBar to show your **District Profile** (if you are a District Administrator) or **My School** to show your **School Profile** (if you are a School Administrator). Select **Import** from the **Advanced Settings** menu in the lower right of the screen. The Import Wizard will open in a separate window, displaying the **Select File** screen.

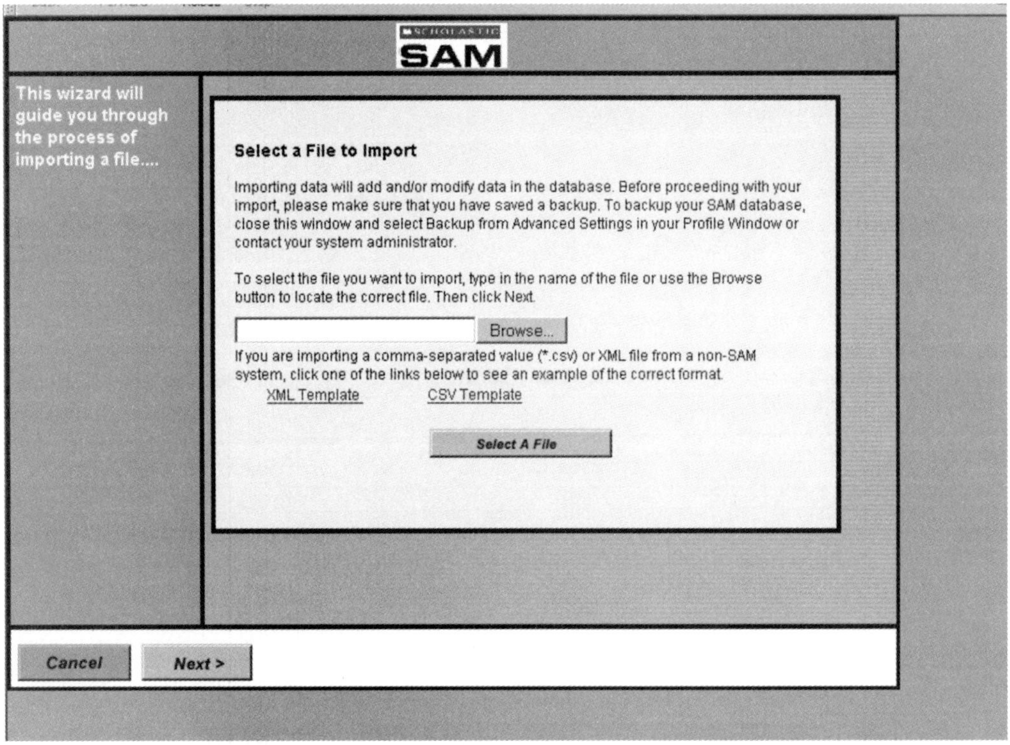

2. Click the **Browse** button to select the file to import. This will open a Windows or Mac pop-up window where you can navigate to the file that you would like to import. SAM will recognize what type of file it is by the extension.

   - If you are importing roster or performance data in the form of an .xml or .csv, you can view the required data format by clicking the **XML Template** or **CSV Template** link.

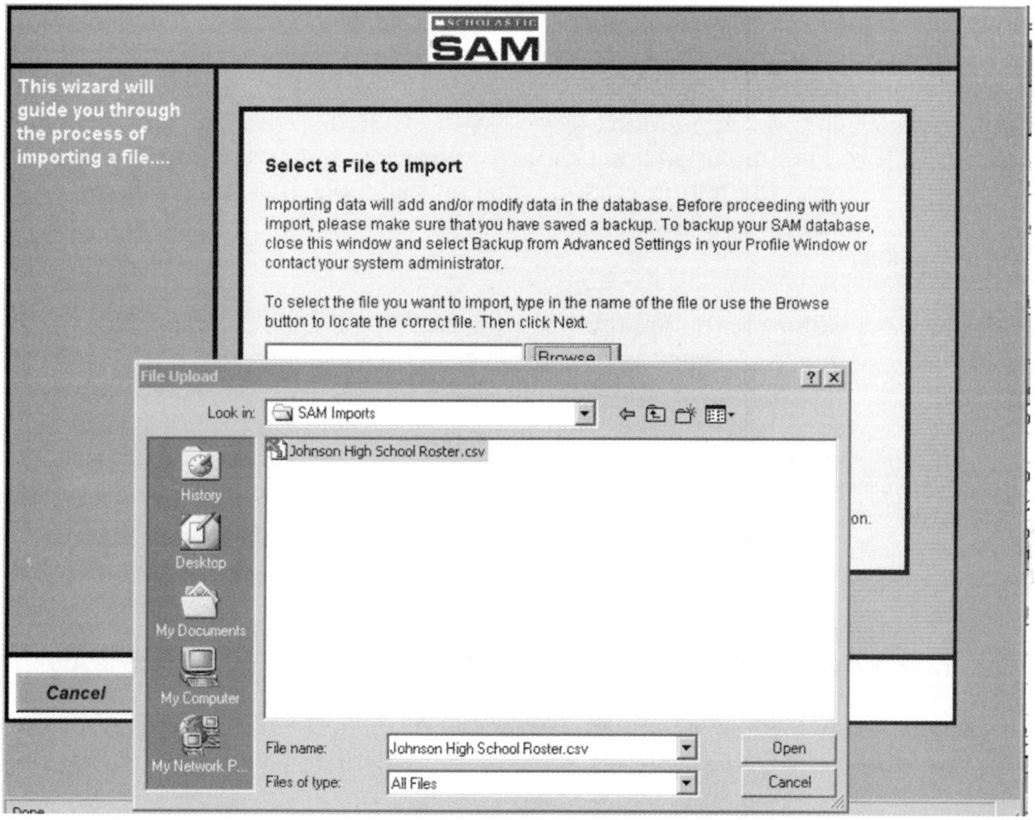

3. Click **Next** once you have selected the file to import. The **Confirm File** screen will display, detailing what type of file you have selected to import (i.e., Student Roster Data, aggregation file, etc.).

4. Click **Import** to proceed. The **Processing Request** screen will display and your request will begin to process. Close the browser window to return to SAM.

   If you are experiencing problems retrieving a file using the **Browse** button in the Import Wizard, you can manually save the file to the SAM server and use the **Select a Server File** button to retrieve the file:

   - Return to the Import Wizard and click the **Select Server File** button. A **Select a File** pop-up window will appear.
   - Use the pull-down menu to select the file and click **Next**. A confirmation screen will appear, describing the type of file you have selected to import.
   - Click **Import** to begin the import process. A **Processing Request** screen will appear. Close the window to exit the Import Wizard and return to SAM.

5. Once the import is complete, you will receive a notification in the **Message Center** on your Home Page. This may take some time if you are importing a large file. When you receive the notification, you can click the **Show Me** link in your **Message Center** to open a window where you can see a record of your recent data movement activity.

Student data that has been imported will show as **Inactive Accounts** and must be activated before the students may use Scholastic programs. See instructions on activating accounts in the following section.

Possible Error Messages

- **Required Fields Missing**: The record does not have some required information (see table above) and SAM cannot import it.
- **Invalid File**: This occurs when you try to import a file other than *.csv or *.xml (or a *.zip file prepared in a SAM export operation).

Managing Inactive Accounts

Inactive accounts are schools, classes, teachers, groups, or students that exist in the database but are not accessible (or visible on the SmartBar) to the current user.

Whenever you import any student file, the imported data will be found in **Manage Inactive Accounts**. All student data that has been imported must first be activated before students can use Scholastic programs. As an Administrator, you can activate accounts by clicking the **Manage Inactive Accounts** link, which is found in the **Advanced Settings** menu on the **District Profile** screen (if you are a District Administrator) or **School Profile** screen (if you are a School Administrator).

To manage inactive accounts:

1. From your District or School Profile screen, click the **Manage Inactive Accounts** link in the Advanced Settings menu. The **Manage Inactive Accounts** screen displays. This window has a table that displays a list of all accounts (Schools, Grades, Classes, Teachers, and Students) that have been designated as inactive.

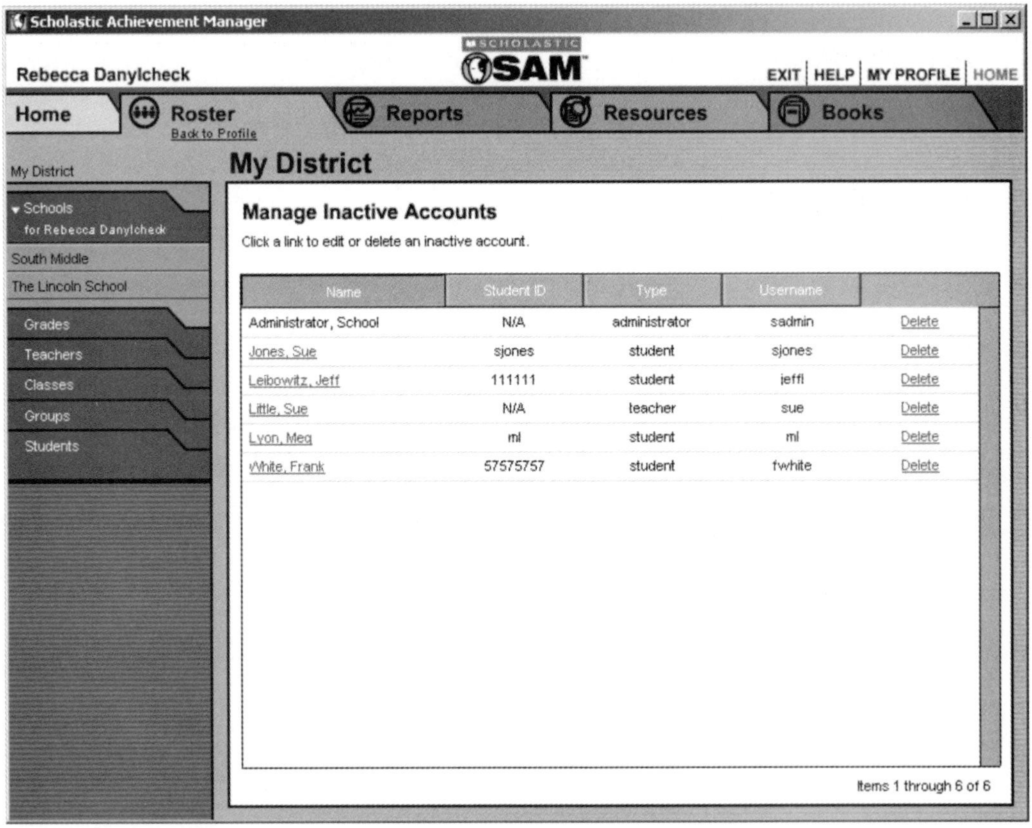

2. Click the link associated with the account **Name** that you would like to activate. For Student and Class accounts, a **Reactivate this Student** (or **Class**) window will open. Other account types will go directly to the **Edit _____ Profile** window. (See example on **page 106.**)

3. Use the pull-down menu on the **Reactivate This Student** (or **Class**) window to select a school to which you would like to associate this account. Then click **Proceed**.

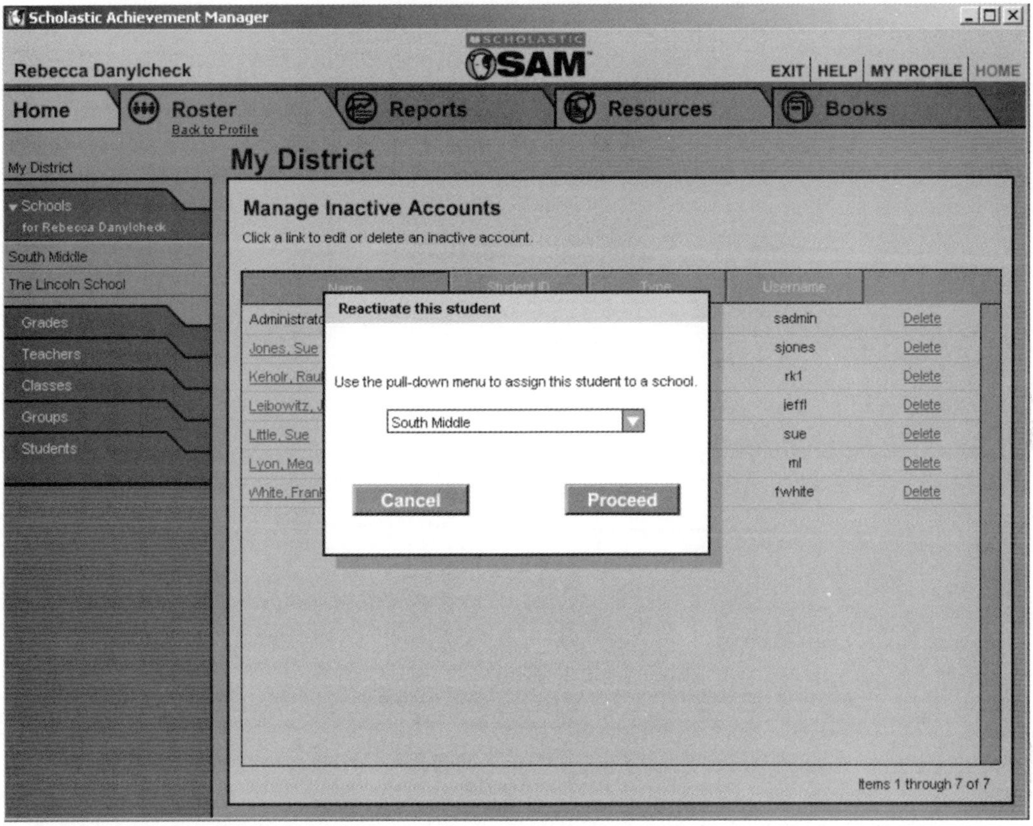

4. The **Edit ______ Profile** window will open.

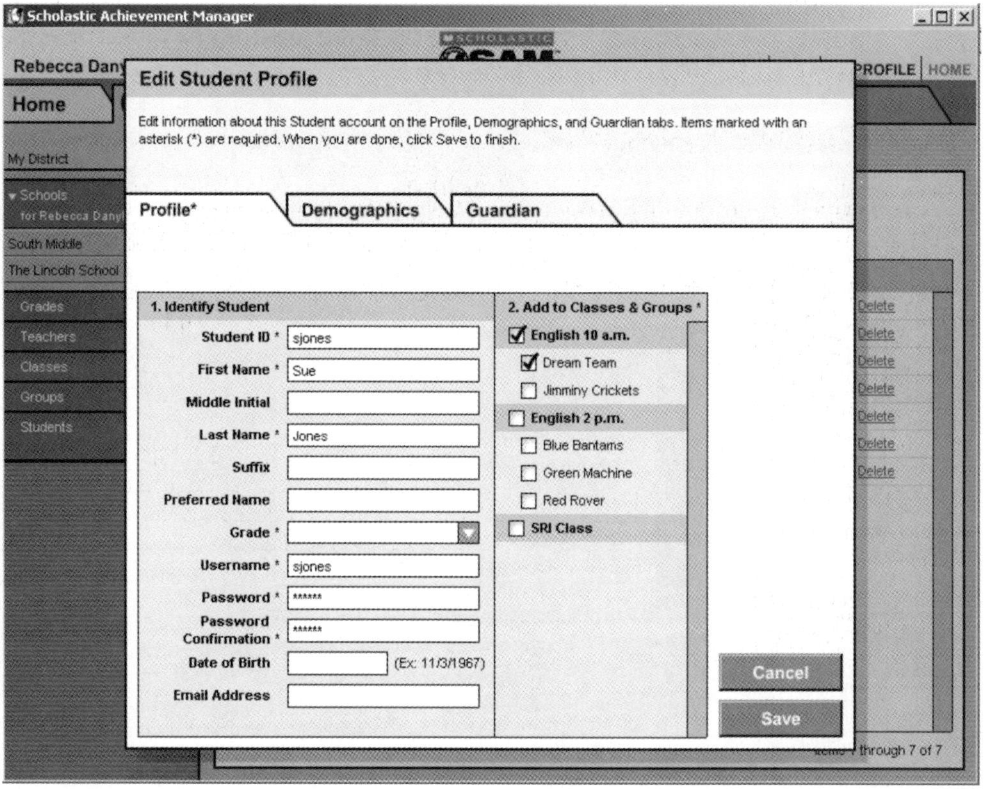

- **Students:** Use the check boxes to associate the student with a class, then click **Save** to reactivate the account. The window will close and you will return to the **Manage Inactive Accounts** window.

- **Teachers:** Teachers must be associated with at least one Class; then click **Save** to reactivate the account. The window will close and you will return to the **Manage Inactive Accounts** window.

- **Schools and Classes:** To reactivate Schools and Classes, simply click **Save** from the **Edit _____ Profile** window. The window will close and you will return to the **Manage Inactive Accounts** window.

When you successfully reactivate an account it will immediately appear in the SmartBar.

5. To finalize the activation process for a student, you must enroll him or her in a Scholastic program. Double-click the student's name on the SmartBar (and click the yellow **Roster** tab if necessary) to bring up the student's profile screen. Then click **Manage Enrollment** under **Manage Roster** in the upper right of the screen.

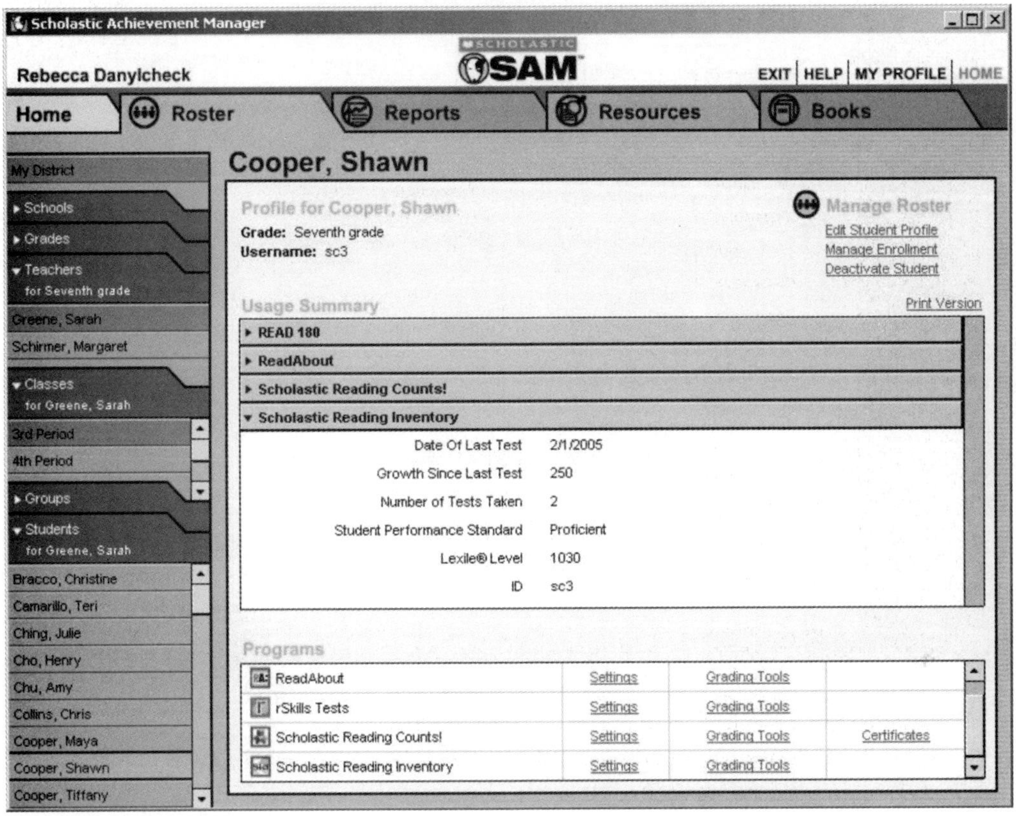

6. The **Manage Enrollment** screen will open. Click the check boxes to select the programs in which to enroll the student.

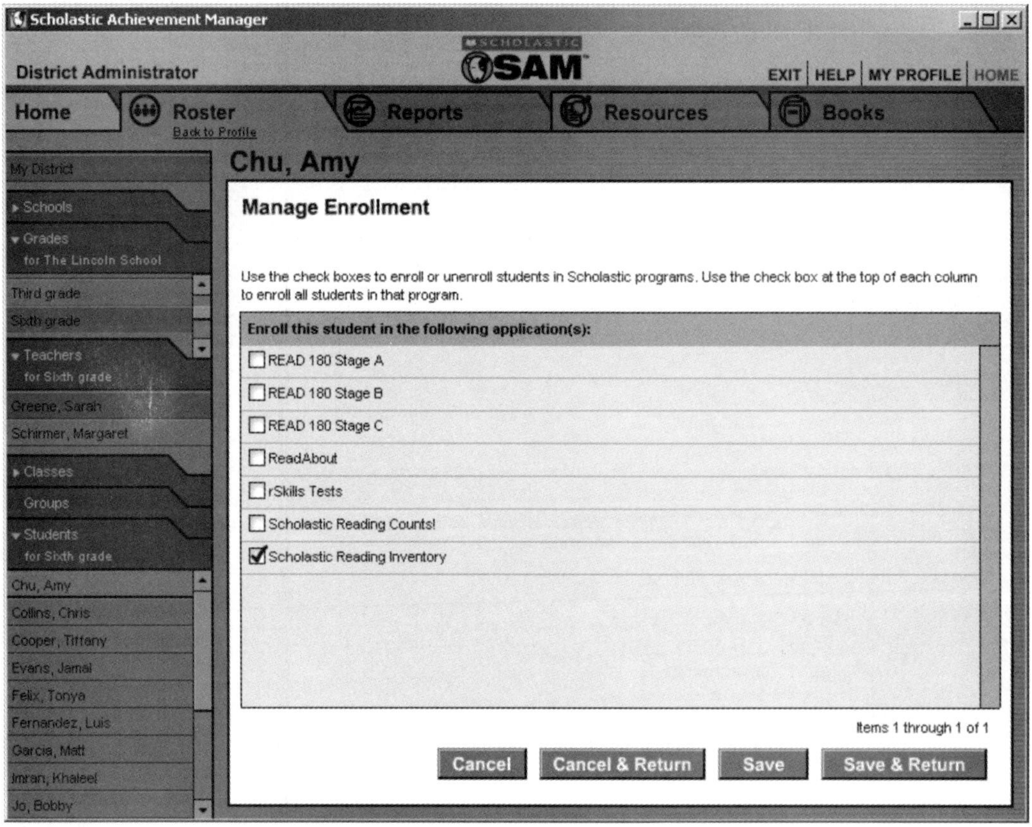

When you are done, click **Save & Return** to close the window and return to the profile screen, or **Save** to save your changes and remain on the **Manage Enrollment** screen. Or click **Cancel** or **Cancel & Return** to close the window without enrolling the student.

More details on enrollment and licenses can be found in the ***SRI Educator's Guide.***

Exporting for Student Transfer

You may transfer student data out of one SAM installation and into another SAM database. The Student Transfer process removes all performance records from the student's current school. It prepares a file you can use to import the data for use in another SAM database—for example, a student moving from a school using one SAM database to a new school using another SAM database. This function may only be performed by a SAM user with administrative permissions.

Students who are transferred are deleted from their existing SAM database, preparatory to being imported into a different SAM installation. If you plan on aggregating data across several SAM installations, using the Student Transfer export when students move is the best way to maintain "clean" databases for aggregation.

To export data for transfer:

1. Perform a database backup before exporting any files.
2. Double-click **My District** at the top of the SmartBar to show your **District Profile** (if you are a District Administrator) or **My School** to show your **School Profile** (if you are a School Administrator). Select **Export** from the **Advanced Settings** menu in the lower right of the screen. The Export Wizard will open in a separate window.

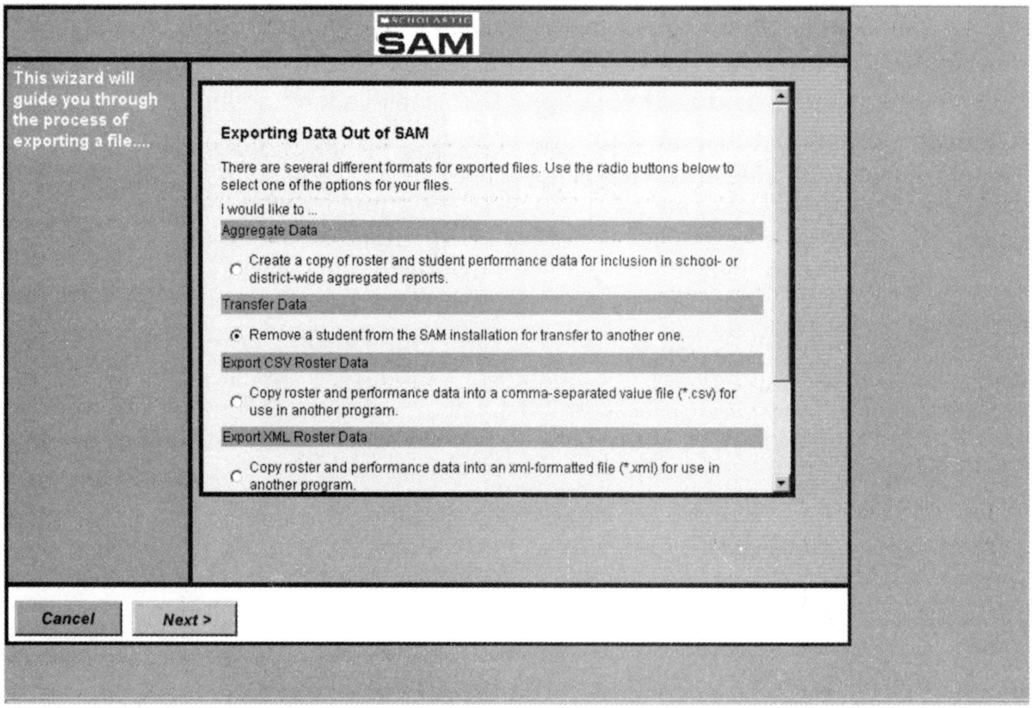

3. Click the radio button to select **Transfer Data** and click **Next**.

4. The **Select Students** screen will display. Use the pull-down menus to select the school, teacher, and classes you would like to transfer out of SAM.

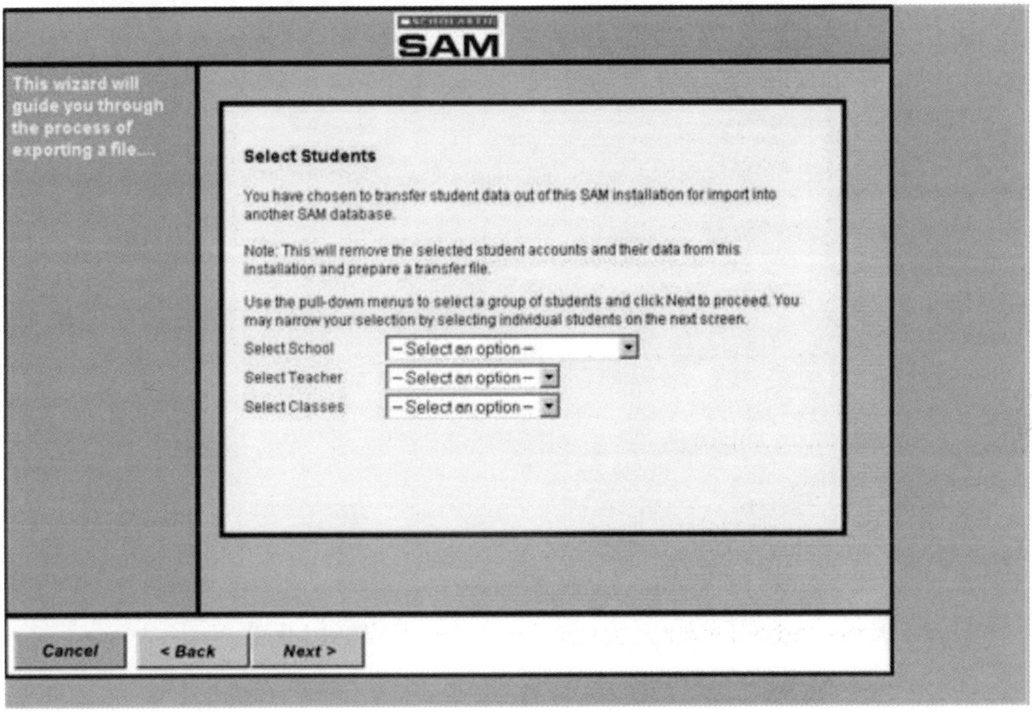

Click **Next** to continue.

5. The **Filter Selection** screen will appear.

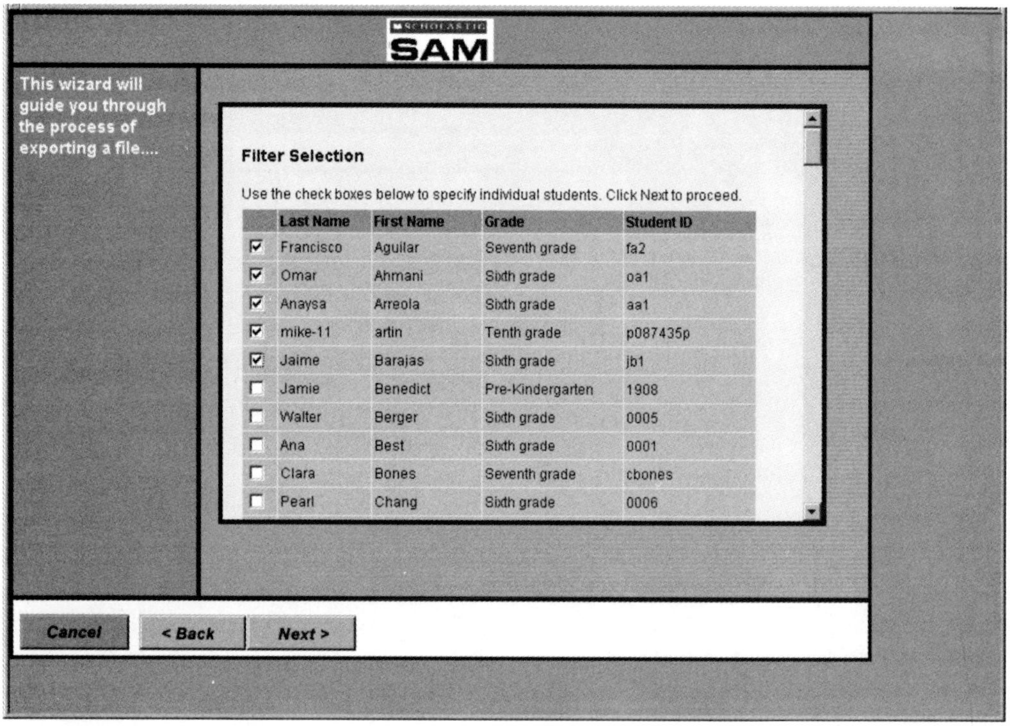

Click the check boxes to select those students you wish to transfer out of this SAM installation. Click **Next** to continue.

6. The **Confirm Selection** screen appears. If you want to change your choices, use the **Back** button to return to the **Filter Selection** screen. Or, click **Next** to continue.

7. Click **Close** to close the browser window and return to SAM. You will receive a notification in the **Message Center** on your Home Page when your export file is ready. This may take some time if you are exporting a large file.

8. You must save this exported file to retrieve it for transferring student data into the new SAM installation. Click the link in your **Message Center** to open the **Show Me** window from which you can save the file to a specific location or to portable media (such as a CD-ROM).

Exporting Student Roster and Performance Data (*.csv or *.xml)

Student roster and performance data can be exported for use in other software programs such as Microsoft Excel or a student information system. You can choose to export files in CSV or XML format. This function may only be performed by a SAM user with administrative permissions.

Data for all students in the SAM installation will be exported. However, the information will be restricted by your time period and program selections.

To export data for use in a different application:

1. Double-click **My District** at the top of the SmartBar to show your District Profile (if you are a District Administrator) or **My School** to show your School Profile (if you are a School Administrator). Select **Export** from the **Advanced Settings** menu in the lower right of the screen. The Export Wizard will open in a separate window.

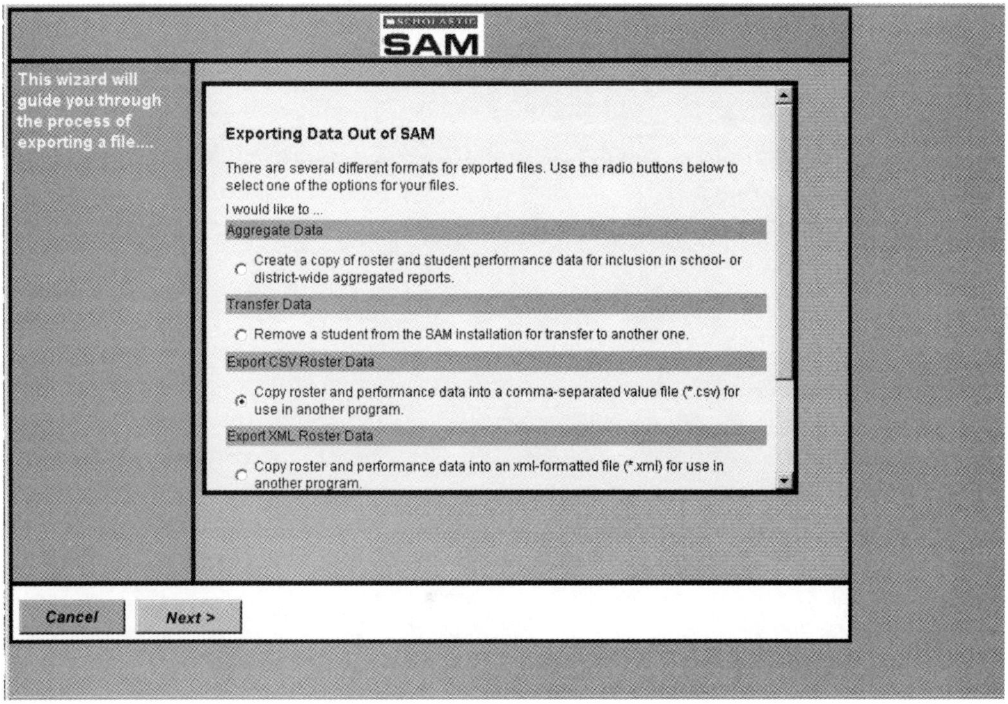

2. Click the radio button to select either **Export CSV Roster Data** or **Export XML Roster Data** and click **Next**. The **Select Students** screen will display.

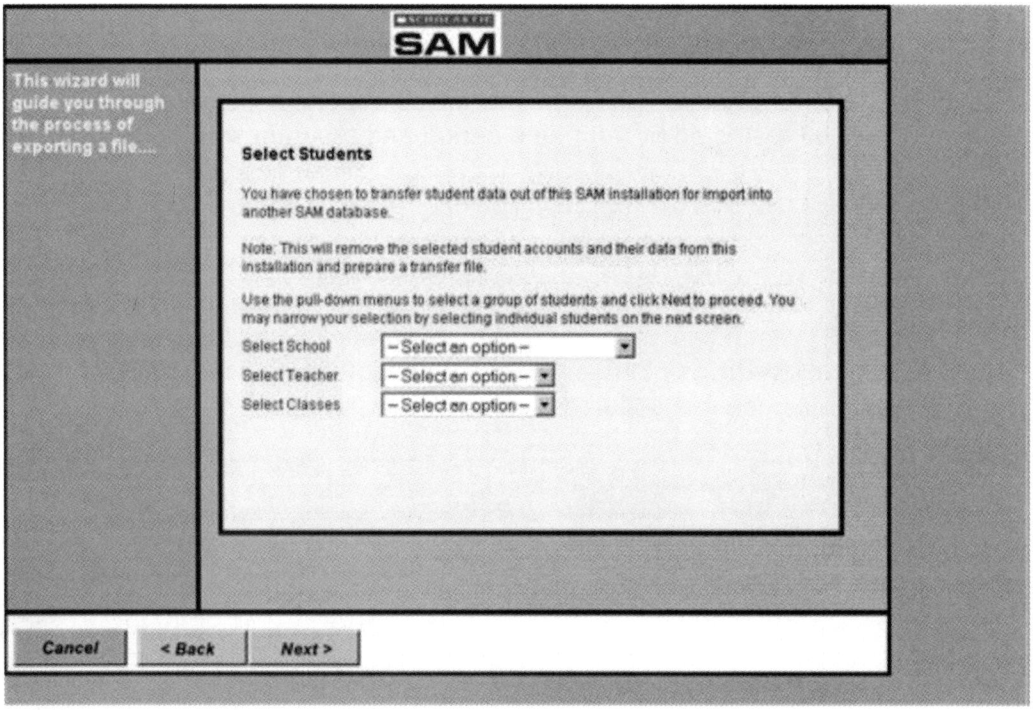

3. Use the pull-down menu to select the school, teacher, and classes for which you would like to export data. Click **Next** to continue. The **Filter Selection** screen will display.

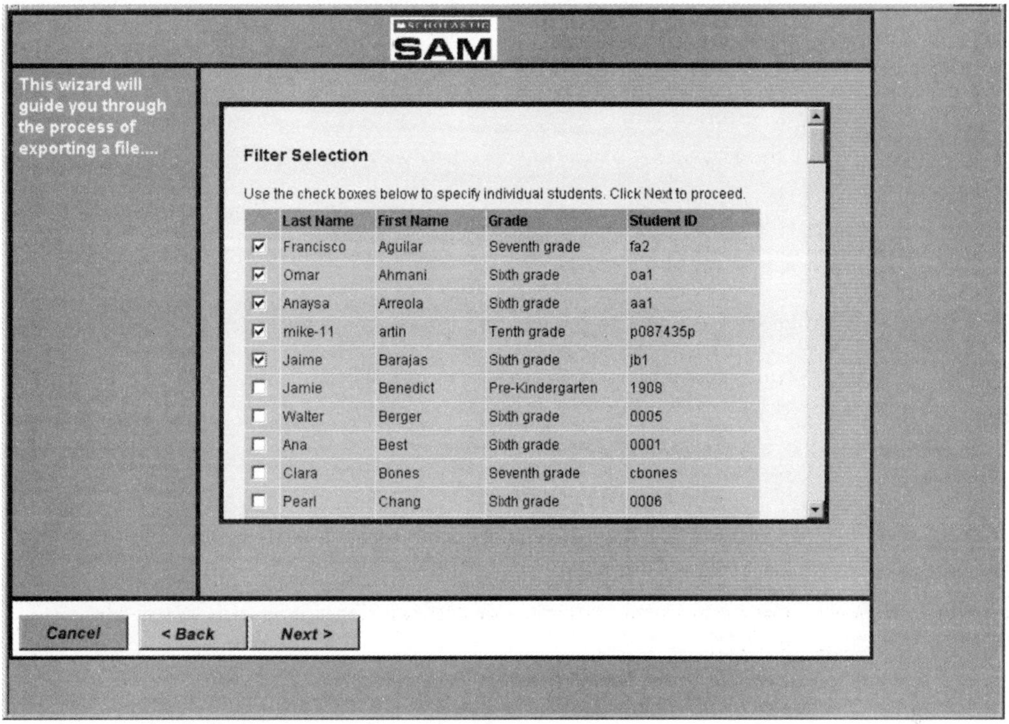

4. Click the check boxes to select those students you wish to transfer out of this SAM installation. Click **Next** to continue.

5. The **Confirm Selection** screen appears. If you want to change your choices, use the **Back** button to return to the **Filter Selection** screen. Or, click **Next** to continue.

6. The **Time Period Selection** screen will appear.

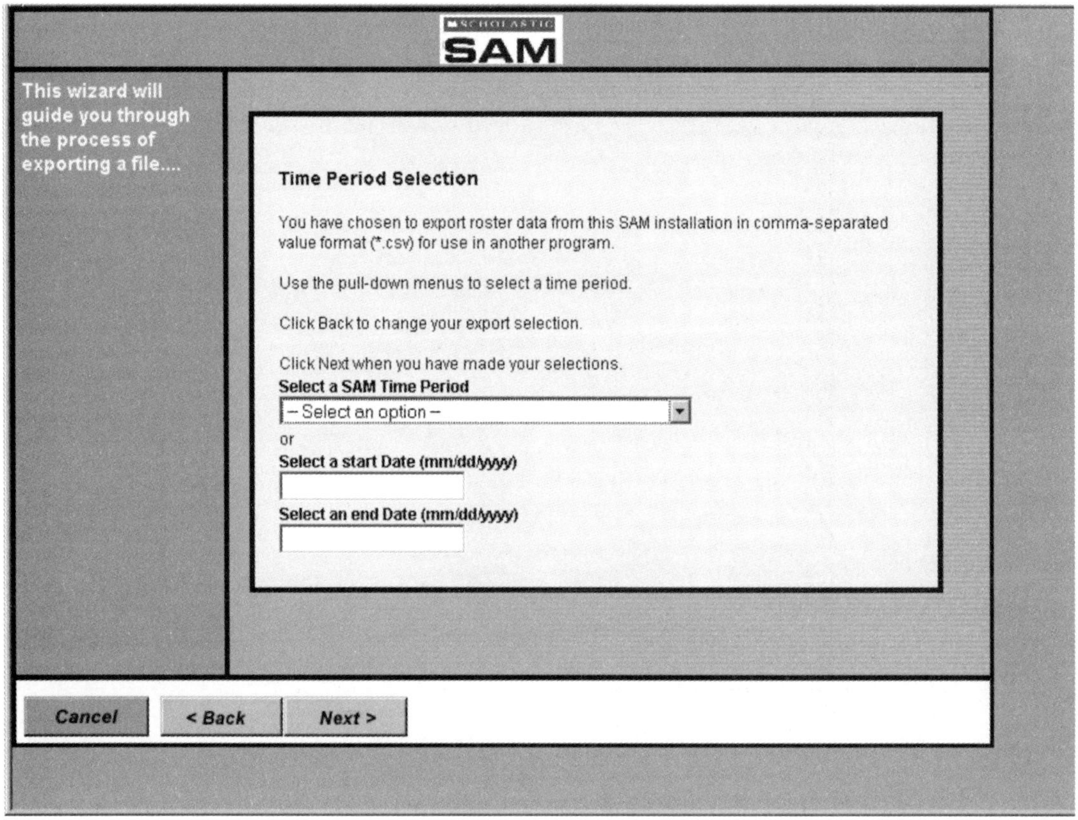

Use the pull-down menu to select a preset time period or enter a start date and an end date. Click **Next** to continue.

7. The **Program Selection** screen will display.

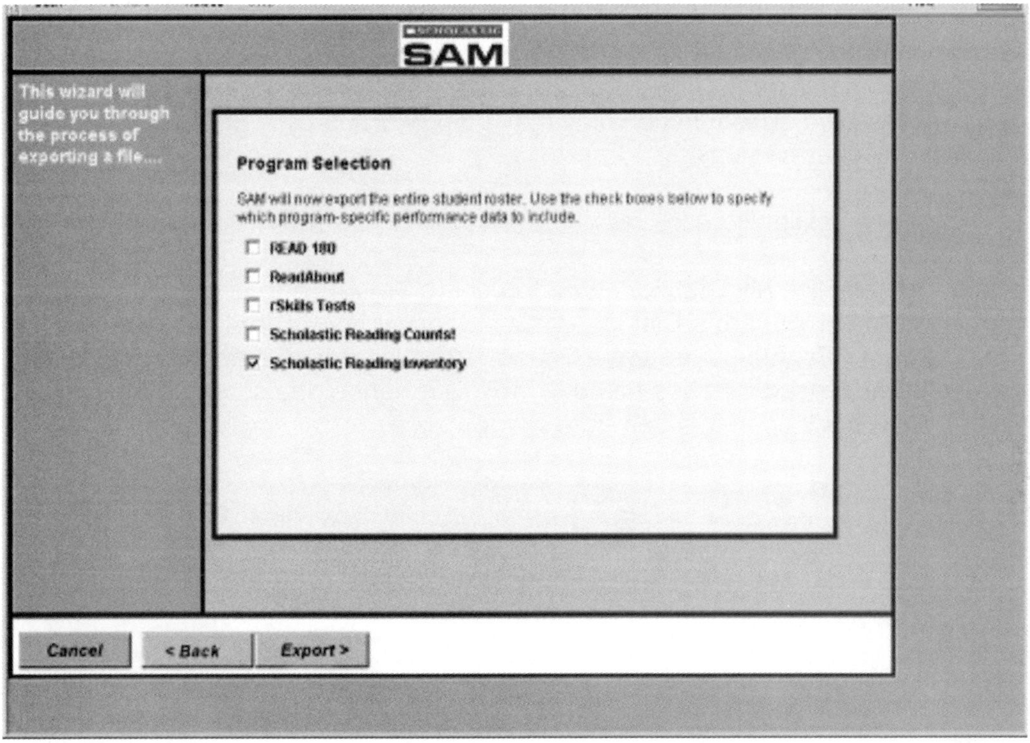

8. Click the boxes to select the Scholastic programs for which you would like to include data to be exported and then click **Export**. The **Processing Request** screen will display and your export request will begin to process. Close the browser window to return to SAM.

9. You will receive a notification in the **Message Center** on your Home Page when your export file is ready. This may take some time if you are exporting a large file.

10. You must save this exported file to retrieve it for later use. Click the link in your **Message Center** to open the **Show Me** window from which you can save the file to a specific location or on portable media such as a CD-ROM.

Exporting SRI Lexile® Data

Student SRI Lexile information can be useful in placing students in Scholastic reading programs, such as ***READ 180*** and *ReadAbout.* The **SRI Lexile Export** function allows this data to be transferred into a SAM installation that does not have SRI installed. This function may only be performed by a SAM user with administrative permissions.

To export SRI Lexile scores:

1. Double-click **My District** at the top of the SmartBar to show your **District Profile** (if you are a District Administrator) or **My School** to show your **School Profile** (if you are a School Administrator). Select **Export** from the Advanced Settings menu in the lower right of the screen. The Export Wizard will open in a separate window.

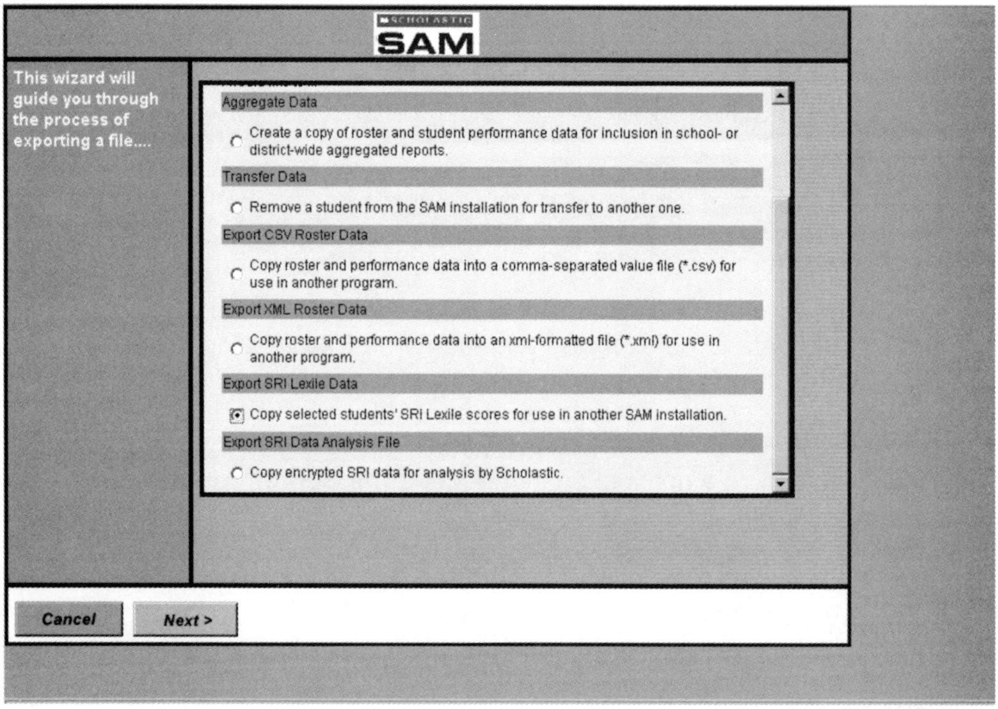

2. Click the radio button to select **Export SRI Lexile Data** and click **Next**. The **Select Students** screen will display.

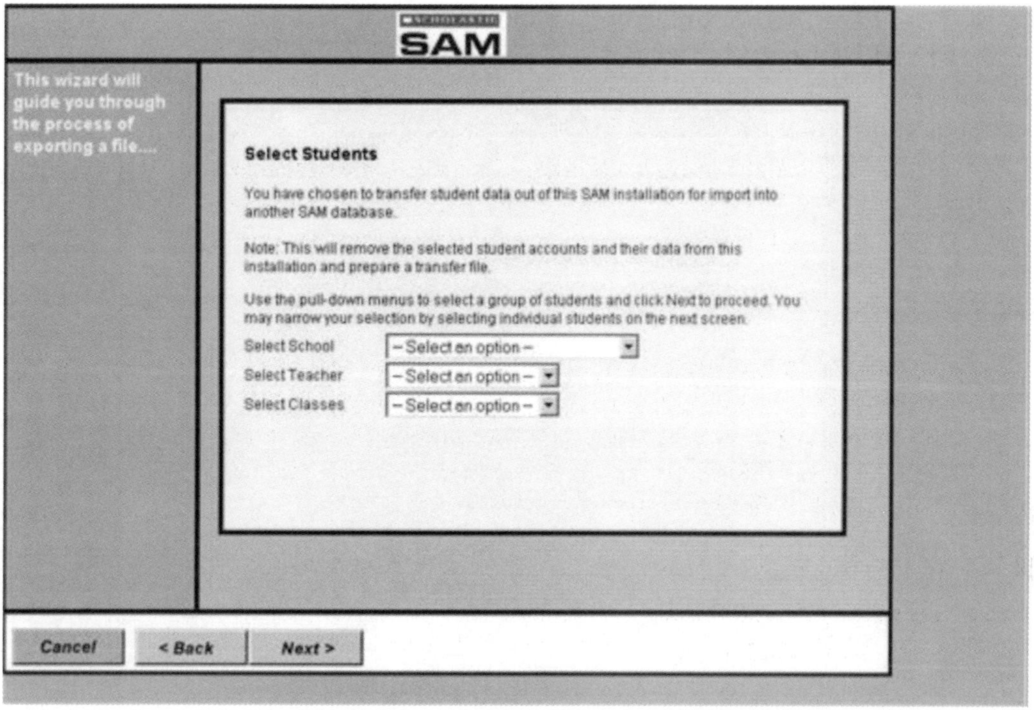

3. Use the pull-down menus to select the school, teacher, and classes for whom you would like to export SRI scores. Click **Next** to continue.

4. The **Filter Selection** screen will appear.

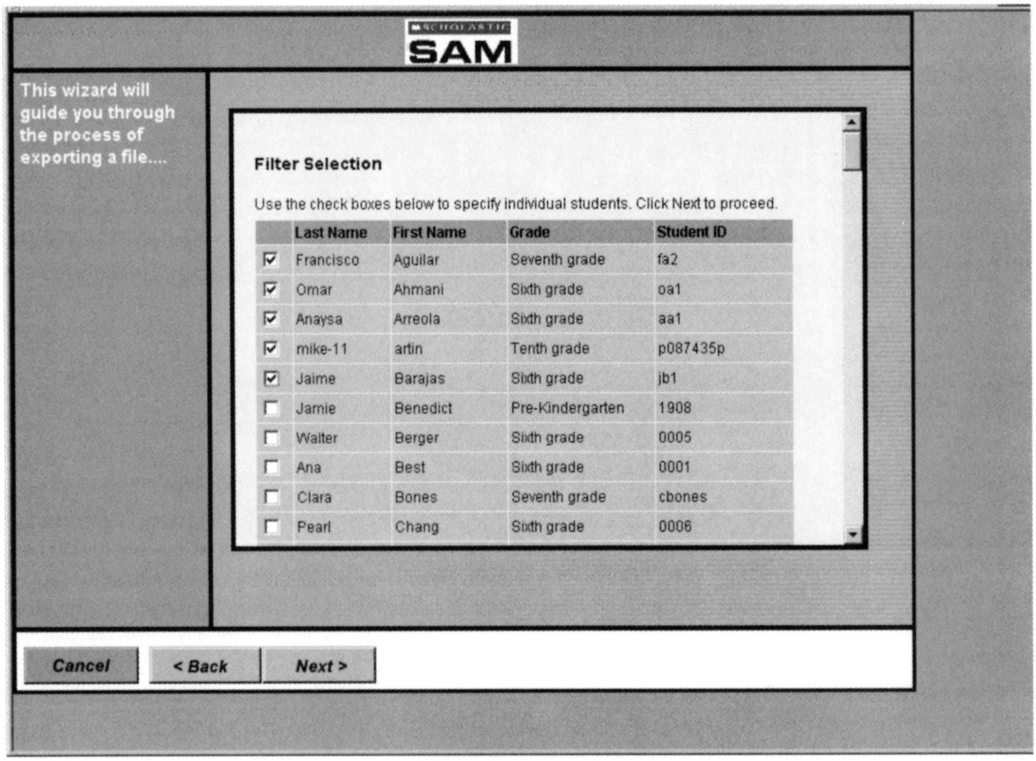

Click the check boxes to select those students for whom you wish to export SRI Lexile scores. Click **Next** to continue and the **Confirm Selection** screen appears.

5. If you want to change your choices, use the **Back** button to return to the **Filter Selection Screen**. Or, click **Export** to continue. The **Processing Request** Screen will display and your export request will begin to process. Close the browser window to return to SAM.

6. You will receive a notification in the **Message Center** on your Home Page when your export file is ready. This may take some time if you are exporting a large file.

7. You must save this exported file to retrieve it for later use. Click the link in your **Message Center** to open the **Show Me** window from which you can save the file to a specific location or on portable media, such as a CD-ROM.

Creating an SRI Data Analysis File

This encrypted file provides a means for Scholastic to evaluate the performance of SRI. The file allows Scholastic to work with some districts to conduct additional evaluations and research on the raw data directly related to the psychometric characteristics of the SRI tests.

This file should only be created at the specific request of a Scholastic Customer Service or Technical Service representative, who will provide you with instructions on how to do so.

BACKING UP AND RESTORING THE DATABASE

As with any database that contains information that is updated regularly, you should back up your files in case of a power outage or damage to the drive on which you save files. A SAM backup saves a record of the entire database at a given moment. It is also good practice to use a third-party backup software to back up the entire SAM Server hard drive. These system backups should ideally be saved onto portable media (i.e., tape or CD-ROM) and stored off-site. Note that if you use third-party backup software you will need to stop the Scholastic MySQL and JBoss services to do a hard drive backup. Appendix D, beginning on **page 164** has instructions for stopping and starting these services.

Backing Up

The backup utility in SAM allows you to select the time when the system will perform the backup.

Important Note: Because it is not possible to perform a successful backup while anyone is using SAM or Scholastic programs, this utility **must** be scheduled for after-school hours.

To back up the database:

1. Double-click **My District** at the top of the SmartBar to show your **District Profile** (if you are a District Administrator) or on **My School** to show your **School Profile** (if you are a School Administrator).

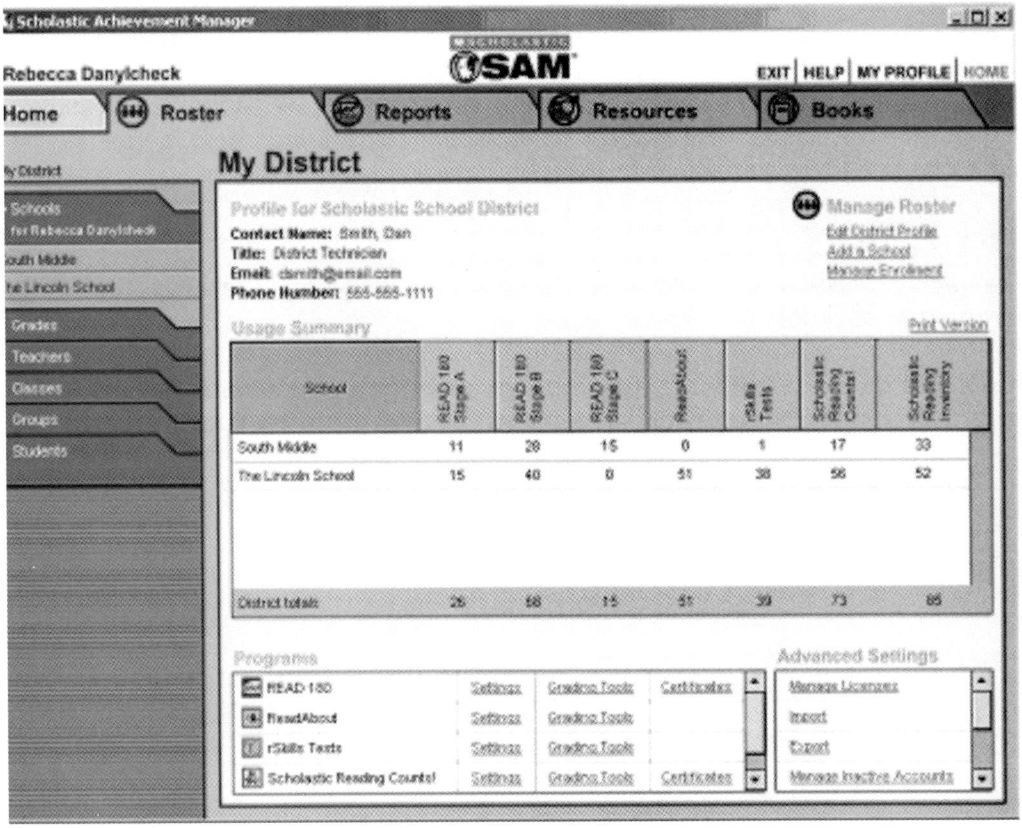

2. Select **Backup** from the **Advanced Settings** menu. The Backup Wizard will open in a separate window.

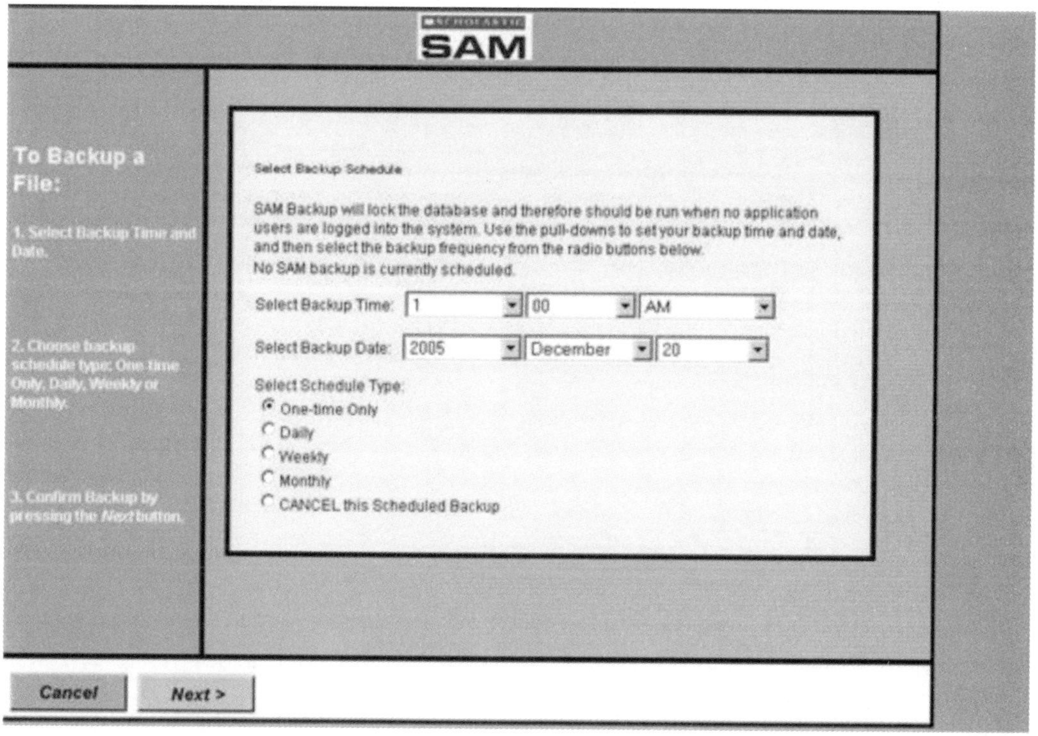

3. Use the pull-down menus to select the time and date at which the backup will begin. Use the radio buttons to select a schedule type for the backup, or to cancel the currently scheduled backup.

4. You will see a screen confirming the time of the backup. Click **Back** to change the schedule, or click **Next** to finish the SAM backup scheduling.

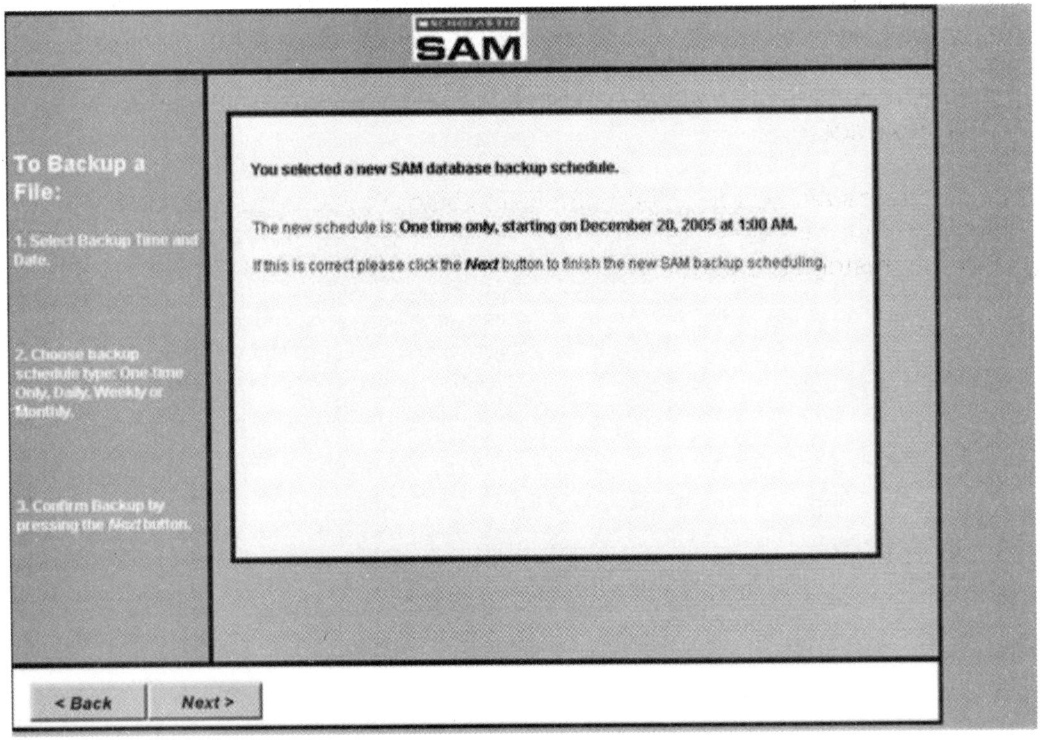

Once the backup is complete, you will receive a notification in the **Message Center** on the SAM Home Page. Close the window to return to SAM.

Your backups are saved to the following location:
C:\ScholasticEE\SAM_Server\jboss\server\lycea\deploy\backup.war

You can also reach backups on the SAM Server by going to:
http://localhost:55880/backup/

Be sure you move your backups to a safe place. The best practice is to save them onto portable media (such as a tape or CD-ROM) that can then be stored off premises.

Restoring

Restoring a database will **write over the current database**. This function should only be performed by the School or District Technical Coordinator and **only** if the current database is lost or corrupted. If your school's database is lost or corrupted, regardless of your SAM permissions, you will see a notification on the SAM Home Page.

Contact Technical Support (1-800-283-5974) before restoring a database containing important student data. They will email detailed instructions on the process for restoring a database.

DATA AGGREGATION

Overview

Data aggregation is the process of unifying data from several different SAM databases within a district to facilitate broad-based reporting. Aggregating the data onto one server gives administrators and reading specialists the ability to run district-wide reports to assess performance and target resources in support of differentiated instruction. Data aggregation is also useful when creating AYP demographic reports to comply with NCLB requirements. This function may only be performed by a SAM user with administrative permissions.

Only data generated from SAM installations in the same district (as indicated by the exact same district name) may be aggregated.

Note: The spelling of the district name ***must be exactly the same*** on each database and on the aggregation server for the data to unify correctly.

Because data aggregation utilizes a snapshot of the data, it is important that data for aggregation be exported when no one is logged on to SAM, and no students are using programs that would try to write to the database during the export for aggregation.

The Data Aggregation Server

A Data Aggregation Server should, at the very least, have a separate SAM installation dedicated to aggregation. It should ***not*** be a server used for a working (live) SAM database, as each time databases are aggregated they replace student and teacher data, and often the entire database is purged prior to aggregation. The aggregation server must be a separate server.

The Data Aggregation Server should meet the recommended system requirements as specified on **page 10**.

You must install the following Scholastic software on the Data Aggregation Server. See the referenced pages for specific installation instructions.

- Disc 1: SAM Server, **page 19**
- Disc 2: SAM Client, **page 30**
- Disc 3: ***SRI*** Server, **page 43** (You must also install all of the Server components for any other Scholastic programs for which you intend to aggregate data—i.e., *READ 180*, Scholastic Reading Counts!, rSkills Tests.)

No licenses are necessary for the Data Aggregation Server, as Scholastic Client software (other than SAM) is not installed and this server should not be used by students or teachers for Scholastic activities.

Exporting Data for Aggregation

The first step of the aggregation process is to export the data. This export is done on the schools' SAM installations. No one (students or teachers) should be using any Scholastic software during the export process.

To export data for aggregation:

1. Double-click **My District** at the top of the SmartBar to show your **District Profile** (if you are a District Administrator) or **My School** to show your **School Profile** (if you are a School Administrator). Select **Export** from the **Advanced Settings** menu in the lower right of the screen. The Export Wizard will open in a separate window.

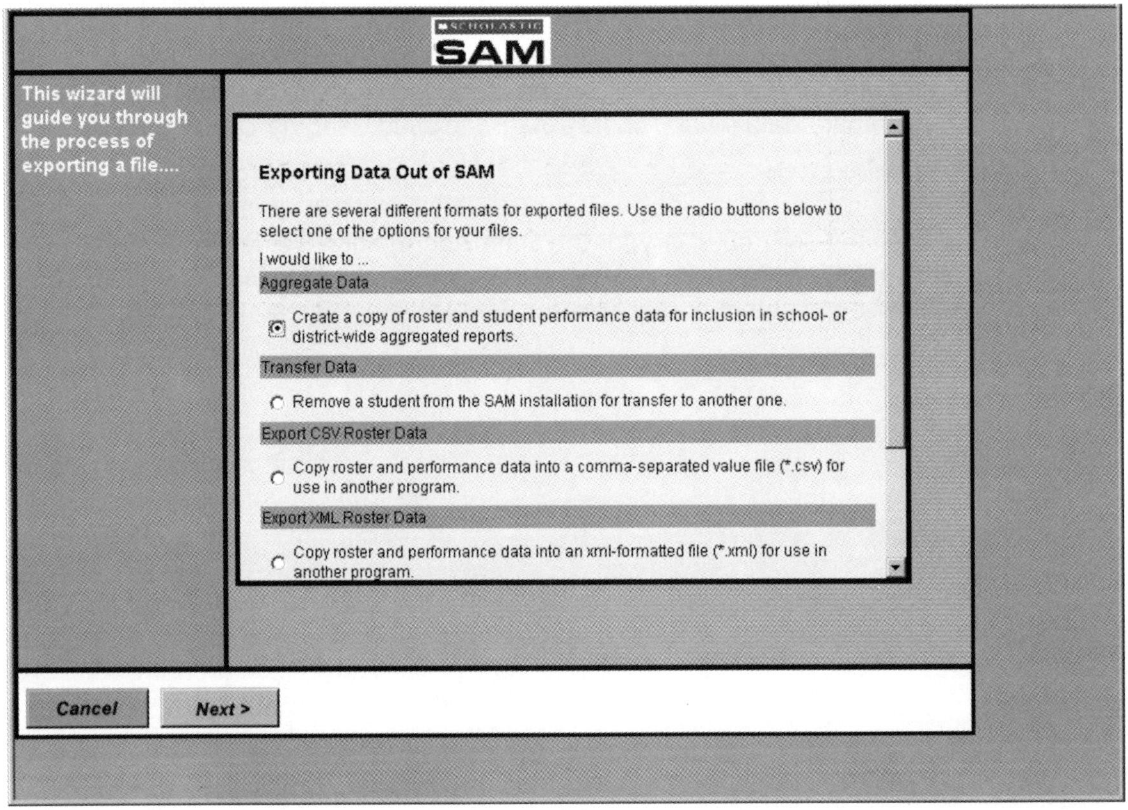

2. Click the radio button to select **Aggregate Data** and click **Next**. The **Program Selection** screen will display.

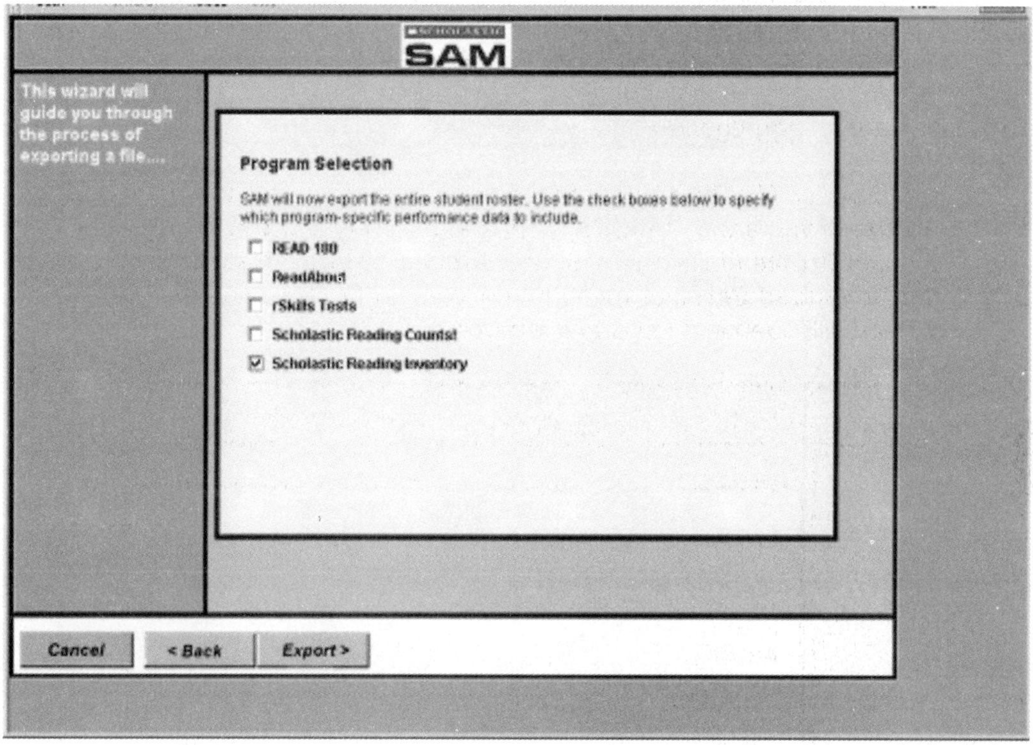

3. Click the boxes to select the programs for which student data will be exported for aggregation. Click **Export** to begin the export process. The **Processing Request** screen will display.

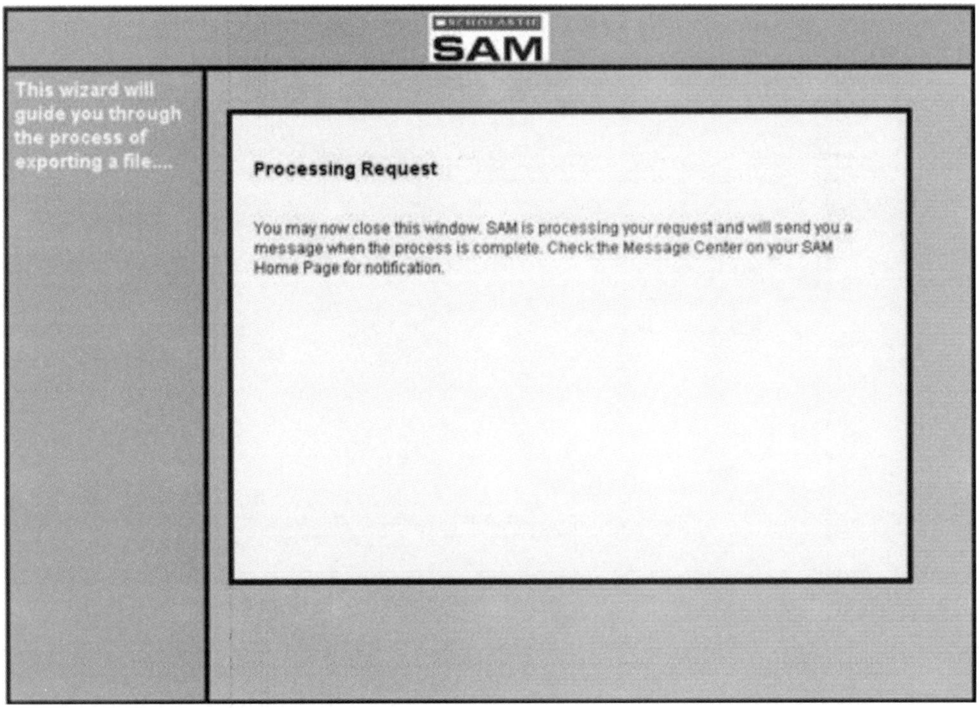

4. Click **Close** to close the browser window and return to SAM.

5. You will receive a notification in your **Message Center** on your Home Page when your export file is ready. This may take some time if you are exporting a large file.

6. You must save this exported file to retrieve it for later use and to move it to the aggregation server. Click the link in your **Message Center** to open the **Show Me** window from which you can save the file to a specific location or to portable media such as a CD-ROM.

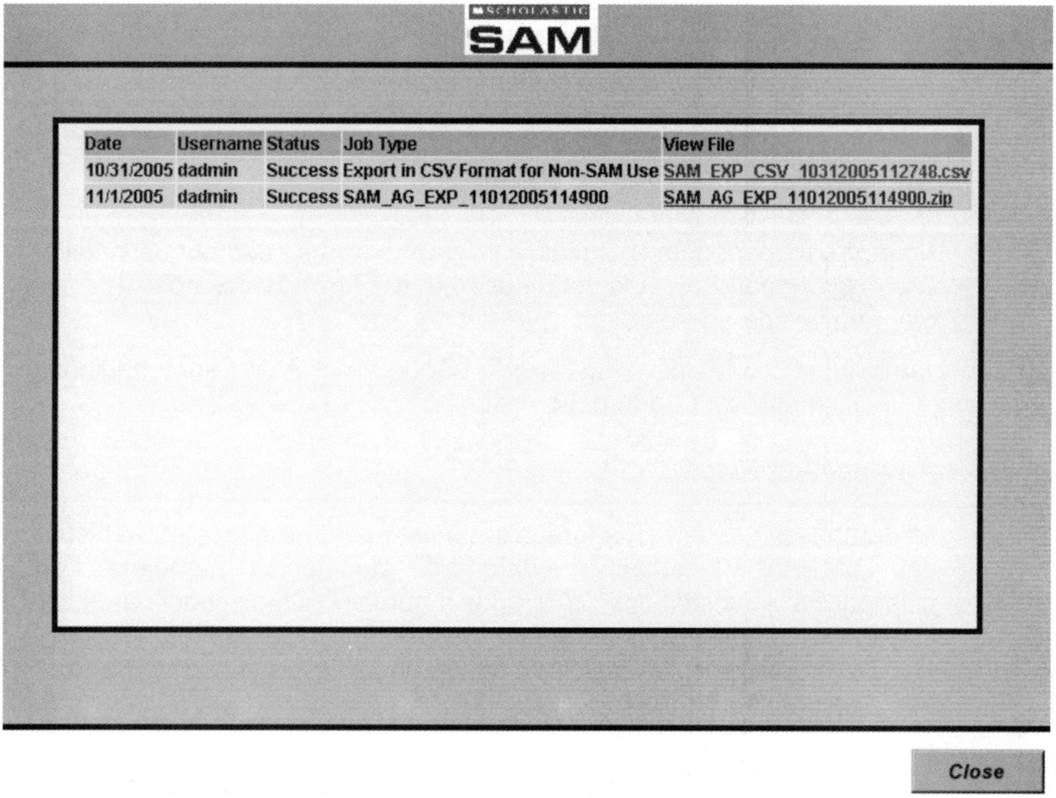

Unifying Aggregated Data

Data is aggregated by importing each of the files that have been exported for aggregation from school SAM Servers onto a designated SAM Aggregation Server at the District level. This aggregation server should have a SAM installation that is solely dedicated to aggregation. It must have:

- SAM Server and SAM Client software installed.
- SRI Server program installed (and Server programs for all Scholastic applications to be aggregated (*READ 180*, Scholastic Reading Counts!, rSkills Tests).
- No active student data (Scholastic Client programs need not be installed). The Aggregation Server is not be used to run any other Scholastic program beside aggregation.

Follow the instructions for installing the SAM Server and SAM Client, beginning on **page 17**, to set up your aggregation server.

Basic Aggregation Rules

- All databases used in an aggregation must have the ***exact same*** district name, or SAM will not unify the data. If the same school name exists on different SAM installations, SAM adds a number to the school name to distinguish the different sources. For example, Lincoln HS1, Lincoln HS2, etc. This change only takes place on the aggregation server; it has no effect on the source data.
- After SAM determines that the database is from the correct district, it next looks for student IDs. Individual student data is unified based on this number.
- If there is a student who has data from the same Scholastic program on two separate databases, the data ***imported onto the Aggregation Server last*** is the data that will appear on the Aggregation Server database.

Possible Aggregation errors include:

- Application Server software not installed: Be sure you have installed the Server software for each of the Scholastic programs that are being used on the SAM installations being aggregated.
- File format not recognized: Be sure you are importing a SAM file that was generated as an export for aggregation.
- Unenrollment never overrides enrollment, so students may appear to be enrolled in programs they are no longer using.

To aggregate data in SAM on the Aggregation Server:

1. Double-click **My District** at the top of the SmartBar to show your District Profile (if you are a District Administrator) or **My School** to show your School Profile (if you are a School Administrator). Select **Import** from the **Advanced Settings** menu in the lower right of the screen. The Import Wizard will open in a separate window, displaying the **Select File** screen.

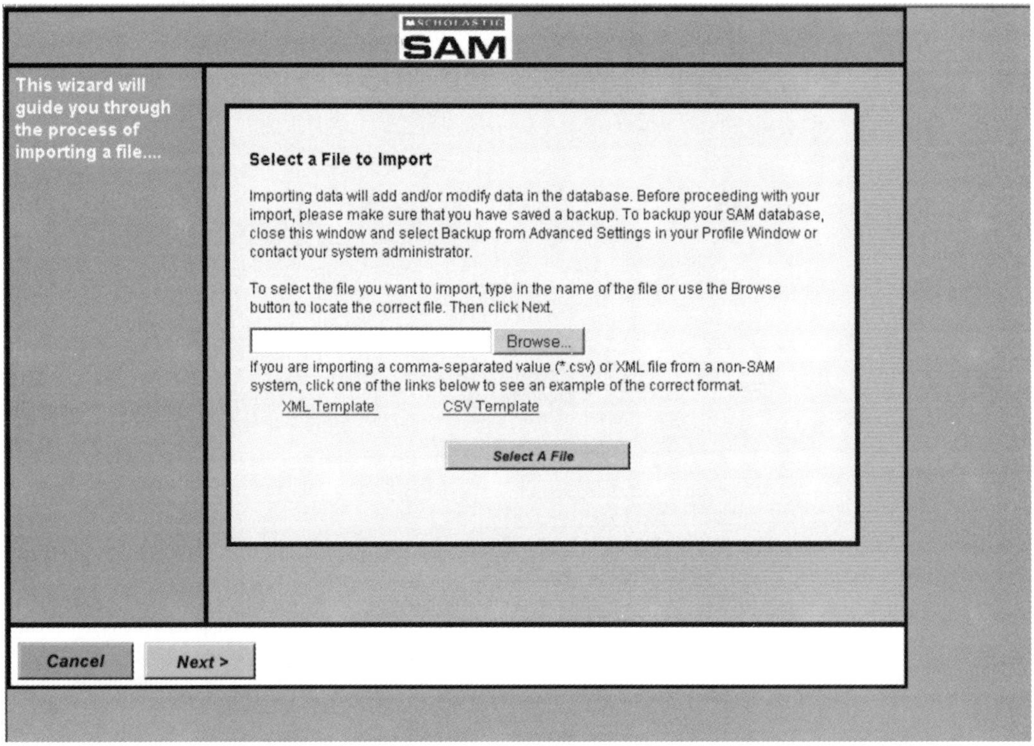

2. Click the **Browse** button to select the file to import. This will open a Windows or Mac pop-up window where you can navigate to the aggregation file that you created.

3. Click **Next** once you have selected the file to import. The **Confirm File** screen will display, confirming that you have selected a .zip file for aggregation.

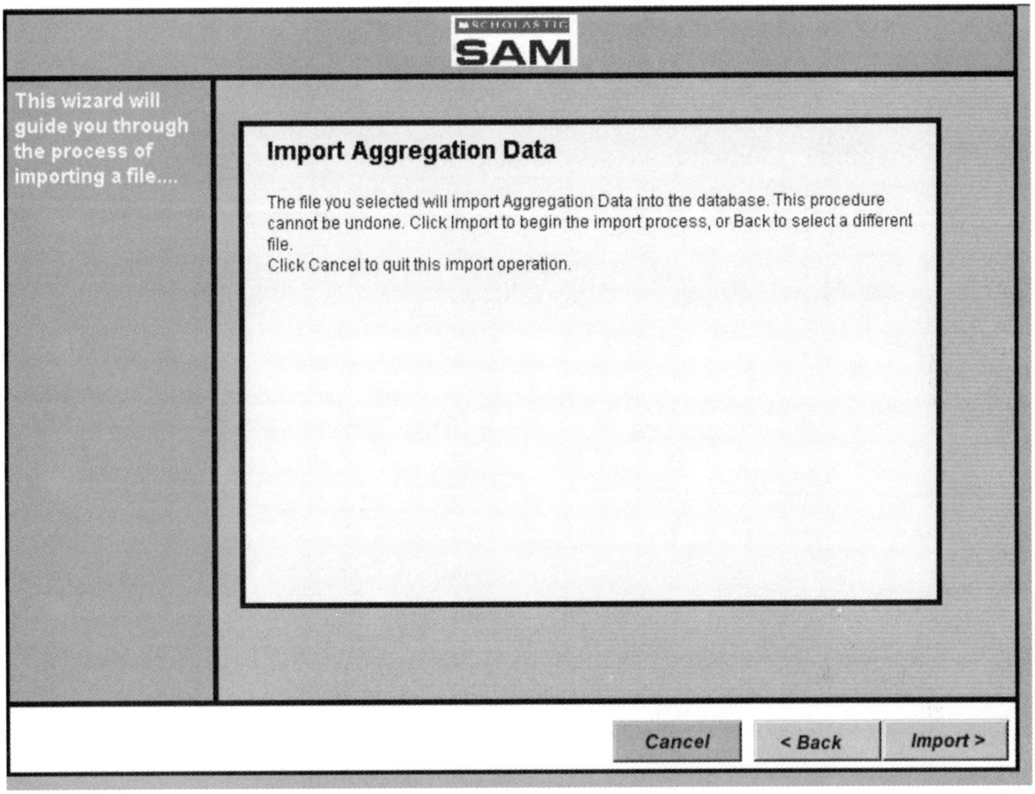

4. Click **Import** to proceed. The **Processing Request** screen will display and your import request will begin to process. Close the browser window to return to SAM.

If you are experiencing problems retrieving a file using the **Browse** button in the Import Wizard, you can manually save the file to the SAM Server and use the **Select a Server File** button to retrieve the file:

- Return to the Import Wizard and click the **Select Server File** button. A **Select a File** pop-up window will appear.
- Use the pull-down menu to select the file and click **Next**. A confirmation screen will appear, describing the type of file you have selected to import.
- Click **Import** to begin the import process. A **Processing Request** screen will appear. Close the window to exit the Import Wizard and return to SAM.

Once the import is complete, you will receive a notification in the **Message Center** on your Home Page. This may take some time if you are importing a large file.

Data Purge on the Aggregation Server

WARNING: Using this utility permanently deletes all data from your database. Be sure this is what you want to do before proceeding. It is only to be used on the Aggregation Server.

The **Data Purge Utility** is used to clean the aggregation database prior to a new aggregation. The **Data Purge Utility** is designed to purge aggregation servers only and should ***never*** be run on a live school SAM installation with student activity! A data purge is an irretrievable loss of data. Therefore, a backup of the aggregation database should always be made before purging the aggregation server.

Though it is not necessary to purge the aggregation database prior to a new aggregation, it can be helpful in a few specific situations. SAM applies the following rules to aggregating data:

- Most recent import overrides previous data.
- Unenrollment never overrides enrollment. Should a student be unenrolled on a program on one SAM Server, and be enrolled in a different program on another SAM Server, when the database is aggregated, the student will appear as enrolled in both programs. If you anticipate this situation, you should use the **Data Purge Utility**.

To run the **Data Purge Utility**:

1. After backing up the aggregation data (see **page 123** for instructions on running a backup), double-click **My District** at the top of the SmartBar to show your **District Profile.** (This function is only available to District Technicians and School or District Administrators.) Select **Data Purge Utility** from the **Advanced Settings** menu in the lower right of the screen. The **Data Purge Utility** will open in a separate window.

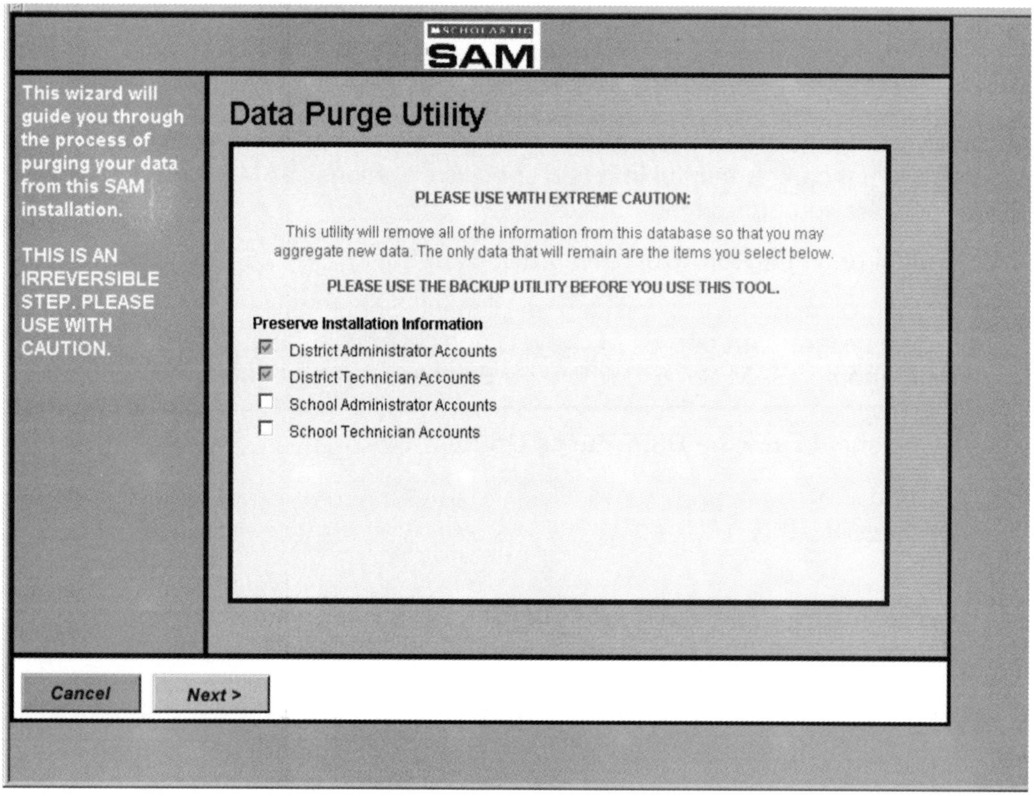

2. The District Technician and District Administrator accounts will always be preserved after a data purge. You also have the option to preserve School Technician and School Administrator accounts. Click the accounts you wish to preserve and click **Next**.

3. The warning screen will appear prompting you to back up the data before continuing. The next step is irrevocable. If you are absolutely certain that you wish to purge data on the aggregation server, click **Next** to start the purging process.

Once you have purged the data on the Aggregation Server you can then begin the aggregation process.

Important Note: Never run the Data Purge Utility on a live SAM database. It will delete all of the data!

TROUBLESHOOTING and FAQs

Installation Issues

Windows

Q: On Windows XP SP2 and Windows Server 2003, why do I get a security-warning message right after selecting and accepting the IP Address screen? The message states “Windows Security Alert” and “Do you want to keep blocking this program?” and lists the program “javaw.”

A: The Installers are built using Java and need to run a Java environment to install SAM EE products. For SAM EE, the installers check each port (55880~55887) for availability. You should select “Unblock” to proceed.

Installation Stalls Without Explanation

Q: The installer froze during installation. What information should I gather before calling Scholastic Customer Service?

A: At the first sign of an installer freezing, please try to:

1. Capture the complete set of logs (installation as well as server). These are:
    - <root-drive>:\ScholasticEE\SAM_Server\log\ [zip up all files in this directory, include the jboss.* files]
    - <root-drive>:\ScholasticEE\SAM_Server\jboss\server\lycea\log\ [zip up all files in this directory]
    - <root-drive>:\ScholasticEE\SAM_Server\mysql\data\localhost.err
    - <root-drive>:\ScholasticEE\SAM_Server\ [all files ending in .log]

2. Capture the current process list (task manager on Windows, or type **ps auxw** in the Terminal on Mac OS X.)
3. Take a screenshot of the installation step on which the installer is frozen.
4. Call Scholastic Technical Support at 1-800-283-5974.

Q: Why does InstallAnywhere installer executable start up and then simply goes away (stops) without a message? When I double-click on the .exe, the same thing happens.

A: On Windows XP SP2 and 2003, DEP (data execution prevention) may prevent an InstallAnywhere executable from running. When this happens, the application will silently be stopped by Windows and no error message will be displayed. The Windows Event Viewer will contain an error message, which can be confirmed by doing the following:

1. **Start → Settings → Control Panel → Administrative Tools → Computer Management →** (in navigation window).
2. Click **Event Viewer →** click **Application**. In the right panel, you should see an entry with "Error" in the **Type** column, and "Application Error" in the **Sources** column.
3. Double-click on the row to bring a pop-up window showing the error message. The **install.exe** should be listed.

To allow installation to continue, DEP must be restricted to Windows programs and services. After installation, this can be changed back, or left as is. To restrict DEP to Windows programs and services, do the following:

1. Click **Start**.
2. Select **Settings → Control Panel → System.**
3. Click the **Advanced** tab. In the **Performance** region select **Settings.**
4. Click the **Data Execution Prevention** tab in the dialog box that opens.
5. Change to use DEP only for Windows programs and services:
    a. Select **Turn on DEP for essential Windows programs and services only.**
    b. Click **OK.**
    c. Reboot the machine.
    d. Upon machine restart, you may get a series of DEP messages; top line listing descriptions such as "Data Execution Prevention—Microsoft Windows" and "InstallAnywhere Self Extractor." Click "Close Message," "Don't Send," or other exit-message type button to proceed.
6. Run the Scholastic Enterprise Edition Installers.
7. Optional: Change the DEP settings back to their original settings.

More information (covering XP, SP2 but also applies to Windows Server 2003) visit:
http://www.microsoft.com/technet/prodtechnol/winxppro/maintain/sp2mempr.mspx

Macintosh Installation Errors

Q: When I try to install ***SRI*** Clients on Mac OS X, why do I get an error about not having Mac OS 9 installed?

A: Open the ***SRI*** Client Install CD (Disc 4) and open the **SRI_Client** folder, expand the Mac OS X folder, and run Install from there.

Install Folder Selection and Creation

Q: If I choose a different location to install SAM than the one suggested during the install process, will the Scholastic folder still automatically be created?

A: The **SAM_Server** directory will always be created. **SCHOLASTICEE**, which is the default directory that's created during a standard install, is replaced with whatever you navigate to or enter. Underneath that will always be a **SAM_Server** directory.

Jagged Logo Appearance on Reports

Q: Why does the product logo have rough edges on PDFs of reports?

A: This is an Adobe Reader issue and can be resolved by opening up this application.

1. Select **Preferences**.
2. Select **Smoothing**.
3. Check the **Smooth Line Art** check box.

Note: This setting is located under different submenus in different versions. It is under **Page Display** in Adobe Acrobat 7. You may need to use Adobe Reader Help to locate this setting.

Security, Firewalls, and Proxies

Q: How does SAM work with firewalls?

A: Firewalls work primarily on ports and IP addresses to protect unauthorized access to your network. Rules for firewalls should be set up to allow SAM to access the server on the selected port. SAM requires the ability to communicate on port 55880 (or another port of your choice). This port must be accessible through your firewall software or hardware.

System Backup

Q: How often should I back up my SAM data?

A: Ideally, we recommend that schools use a 2-step backup process: A weekly backup using the SAM Backup utility, and an additional regular backup of the SAM Server hard drive using external backup software. Backup with external software requires that you shut down the ScholasticMySQL and ScholasticJBoss services; see Appendix D beginning on **page 164** for instructions on shutting down and restarting services.

Q: Is a system backup sufficient for backing up my SAM data?

A: Yes, but we strongly recommend that you also use our backup utility to avoid problems that may result from services running during any other type of backup. If you do a regular system backup and want to avoid any possible problems with Scholastic services, you may shut the Scholastic services down for MySQL and JBoss, run a backup, and then restart those two services. See Appendix D beginning on **page 164** for instructions on shutting down and restarting services.

Working Directly with MySQL Database

Q: Can I access the MySQL database and work on the data directly?

A: By far, the best way to access the SAM database is through the SAM Client and student applications. However, from a technical aspect, MySQL is a relational database with a data schema (table spaces, tables, columns, constraints, indexes, permissions, etc), and hence, it is possible to access the database directly to access and update data in an emergency situation. With this said, such a procedure is extremely risky since the database can be corrupted with a simple command. For this reason, it is recommended that this access is *only* done with review and guidance from Scholastic Technical Support.

Architecture

Q: What is the basic architecture of the ***SRI Enterprise Edition***?

A: SAM runs on a physical server, which includes SAM Server software. Each Scholastic program also has a server component (which is the business logic) that sits on top of SAM. The client applications on the workstations use HTTP to communicate with the Scholastic Program Server software, which resides on a physical server.

Q: Can a program's Server-Component (installation Disc 3) be installed on a different computer than the SAM Server?

A: No. Each program's Server-Component is designed to work with a SAM Server on the same physical computer that the SAM Server software is running on.

Reports Timeout

Q: I'm trying to run reports, and I'm getting an error saying the server did not respond. How can I get my reports to run?

A: Some reports take a long time for the server to prepare, exceeding the timeout for communication between the server and the client. You can lengthen the server-response time to reduce the likelihood of a server timeout while running reports.

You can change the timeout by editing the following XML file; any change you make will be a global change, affecting all of the Scholastic programs that run on SAM.

1. On the SAM server, navigate to the **sam_configl.xml** file, located at: **<root drive>\ScholasticEE\SAM_Server\jboss\server\lycea\deploy\slms-static.war\slms\sam_config.xml**

   In that file, there is a section of XML code that contains the timeout information. It looks like this:

   ```
   <setting>
       <name_id>request_timeout</name_id>
       <description>timeout from within SAM client for the first http
       request. Value is in SECONDS.</description>
       <value>120</value>
   </setting>
   ```

2. To change the timeout, edit the number within the <value> tag of the request_timeout property. The default is 120 seconds. If you change it to 240, then the client will wait 4 minutes before deciding that the server never responded and timed out. If no value is set, the client will default to 120 seconds.

Server Connection Issues

Unsuccessful Connection to SAM Server

Q: Upon initial installation of a new SAM Server, I cannot connect the SAM Client to the SAM Server. What could be causing this problem?

A: In decreasing likelihood, the possibilities are:

1. Incorrect domain name, IP address, or port. Verify that you have provided the correct IP address and port name in the **Add Server** window. See **page 38** for details.
2. Installation failed for an unknown reason. Try reinstalling; call Scholastic Technical Support if you are unsuccessful a second time.
3. A firewall is filtering the connections. Be sure your firewall allows you access to port 55880.
4. A proxy server is causing the connections to fail. You may need to change proxy server configuration to include access for SAM Server IP address and port number. You can disable the proxy Server on any client machines.

Users unable to access server

Q: Why do I get a message saying bad data or unable to connect to the server?

A: Possibilities could include the following:

- There is no server entered in the SAM login screen. See **page 38** for instructions on adding a server.
- The IP address was entered incorrectly. Check to be sure your IP address is correctly entered. For instructions on finding your Server IP address, see the instructions below.
- You could be trying to connect to a dynamic IP address. The SAM Server does not support dynamic IP addresses.
- There is no password entered on the SAM login screen. Enter your password and try again.
- Required services aren't running. See **page 164** for instructions on starting Scholastic MySQL and Scholastic JBoss Services.

Q: When I run the student applications, why do I get a **Server not installed** message?

A: Be sure you have installed *each* server component found on Install Disc 3. This will install all of the programs' server software.

Determining Computer IP Address

Q: How do I determine the server's IP address?

A: Windows 98SE:

1. Click the **Start** menu, choose **Run.** Type **command**, then click **OK**.
2. At the command prompt, type **ipconfig** and press **Enter**. This will display the IP address for each network card on your system.

Windows 2000/XP/2003:

1. Click the **Start** menu, choose **Run.** Type **cmd.exe**, then click **OK**.
2. At the command prompt, type **ipconfig** and press **Enter**. This will display the IP address for each network card on your system.

Mac OS X:

1. From the desktop, click the Apple menu icon on the upper left-hand corner of the screen.
2. Click **About this Mac**.
3. Click **More Info**.
4. On the left-side navigation, click **Network**.
5. The IP address will be listed in the lower-right window.

Changing the Server IP Address that Clients Point To

Q: How do I change what server a client points to? For example, our school has changed the SAM Server static IP address, or the ***SRI*** Client should now be pointing to a different SAM Enterprise Edition Server for this semester.

A: There is a preferences tool for each of the Scholastic client programs that makes it easy to change the IP address and server that the client points to.

To access the **preferences tool**:

1. Using Windows Explorer (or Apple Finder), navigate to the folder containing the Scholastic program for which you would like to make a change. For example, for ***SRI***, go to: **C:\Program Files\Scholastic Enterprise\SRI\SRI Preferences** and double-click to open the Preferences tool. On a Mac, go to: **/Applications/Scholastic Enterprise/SRI/SRI Preferences**

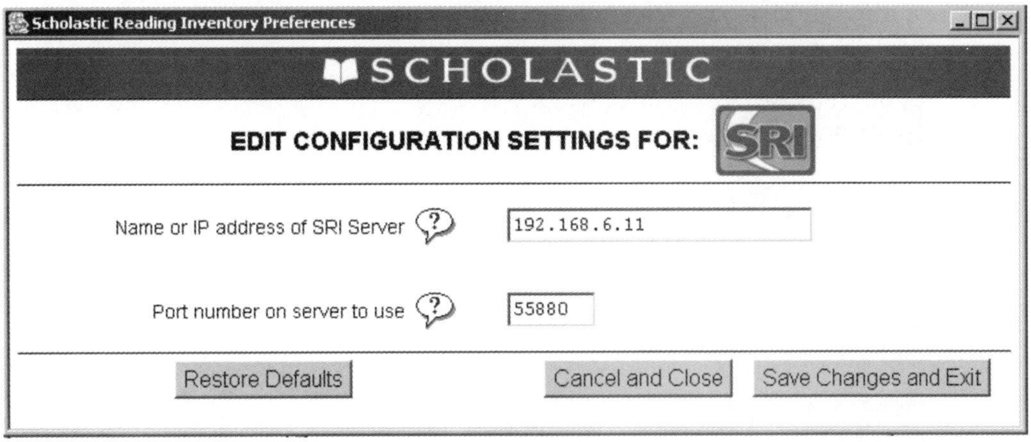

2. Edit the IP address or the port number. When you're done, click **Save Changes and Exit** to save the new IP address and exit the Preferences tool.

Determining Software Version

Q: How can I determine what version the SAM Server and its installed products are?

A: All this information can be found by using the SAM Client. To access this information, do the following:

1. Start the SAM Client and log in to the SAM Server that you want to determine version number(s) for.
2. The first page displayed should be the Home Page. At the bottom of the page you should see a link titled "You are connected to: [your SAM Server's name here]. Click this link to open the **System Information** window.

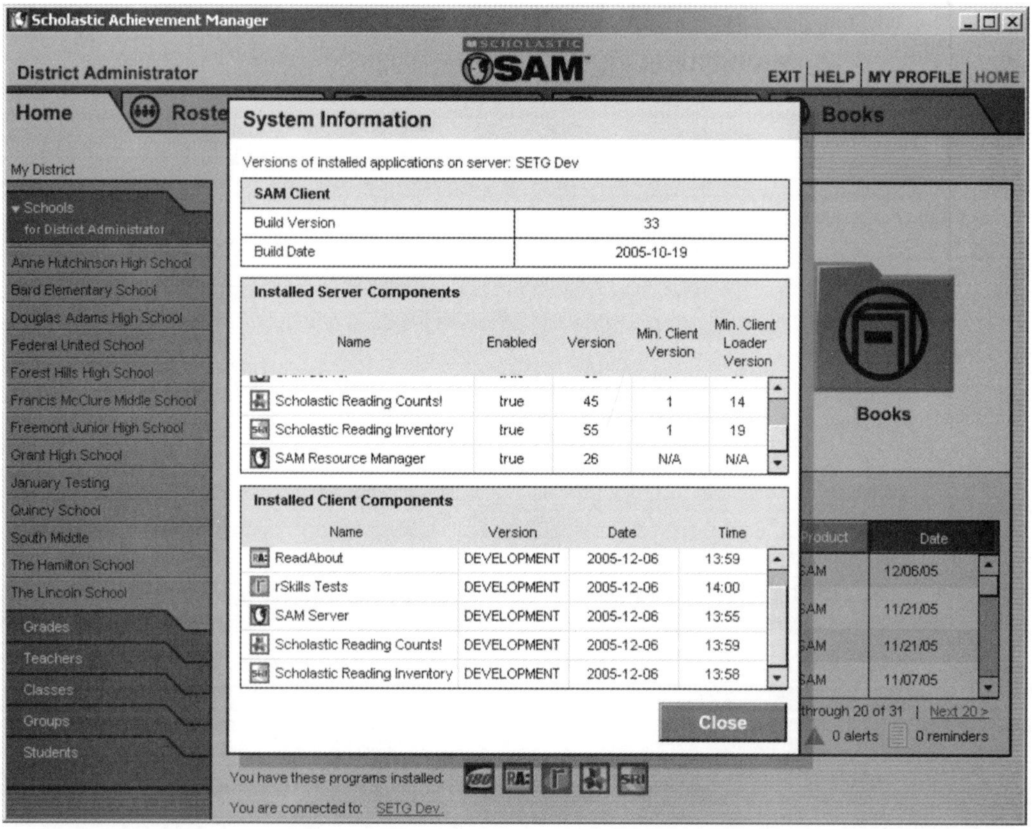

3. There are three sections with version numbers:

   SAM Client

   - This is the version of the SAM Client executable, located on the workstation you are currently using.

   Installed Server Components

   - This is the version of the SAM Server and product Server Components installed on the server you have pointed your SAM Client to.
   - Server Component runs the business logic for each product that is run on the server and with the SAM Server software.

   Installed Client Components

   - This is the version of the Client Code that is held on the SAM Server.
   - Client applications store code in two locations; both locations are used together to create a working client application.
     - The first location is the client code stored on the SAM Server and is downloaded to the workstation when the workstation application is started. The version number displayed here is for this Client Code held on the SAM Server.
     - The second location is the client code stored on the workstation; this code is the Client "Loader" program. For most products this Loader code includes simple logic to connect to a SAM Server and download the Client Code stored there.

Determining Client Software Version Information

Q: How can I determine what version of the Client is running?

A: "Client" in this question means the Client "Loader" program, which is the executable program on each workstation that is used to connect to the SAM Server. To find a Client Loader version number, do the following:

SAM Client:

1. Start application.
2. On login screen, click on the **About SAM** link located below the **Sign In** button.
3. A pop-up window will display showing the SAM Client version number and data.

***SRI* Client**

On Windows:

1. Open Windows Explorer.
2. Navigate to the ***SRI*** Applications folder.
    - Example: <root-drive>\Program Files\Scholastic Enterprise\SRI
3. Click on ***SRI*** executable.
4. Right-click, select **Properties**, select the **Summary** tab.
5. The pop-up window will display a version number in the **Revision Number** field.
    - Example: "Enterprise Edition v1.0.1"

On Mac (both OS X and Classic):

1. Open the Application Finder.
3. Navigate to the ***SRI*** Application folder.
    - Example: <root-drive>/Applications/Scholastic Enterprise/SRI
4. Click on ***SRI*** executable.
5. From the **File** menu, select **Get Info**.
6. A pop-up window will appear listing information about this application. Note the "Version" Information in the **Comments** field.
    - Example: "Enterprise Edition 1.0.1"
    - **Note:** Unlike the other products, a build-number will not be part of the description.

APPENDICES

APPENDIX A: MAINTENANCE

SAM Server and Database Backups

Weekly:

We recommend you schedule a regular database backup using SAM's backup utility, which is found under **Advanced Settings** on an administrator's **Profile** page.

Important Note: If there is server activity, the backup will be faulty and the resultant database backup file may not be usable to restore data. To ensure usable backups, it is important to schedule your backup after working hours when no one will be working on Scholastic programs, so the server will have no activity.

SAM backups are stored at:
<root-drive>\ScholasticEE\SAM_Server\jboss\server\ lycea\deploy\backup.war\SAM_BKUP_[time-stamp].zip

(Time-stamp format is: MMDDYYYYhhmmss)

Alternatively, you can find the backups using an Internet browser on the SAM Server pointed to the following URL:
http://localhost:55880/backup/

Additionally:

You should also use a third-party backup utility to schedule regular backup of the SAM Server hard drive, which includes the SAM database and student recordings.

The files from this backup should be stored on an "external" device (NOT the same hard drive that the SAM Server is running on) such as a tape or CD-ROM. For maximum security, we recommend that these backups be stored off-site. You can use any backup utility that (a) backs up files, directories, and subdirectories and (b) is able to restore these files, directories, and subdirectories.

The following steps should be performed/scheduled when doing this type of backup (detailed instructions for stopping and starting the JBoss and MySQL services can be found in Appendix D beginning on **page 164**):

1. Shut down ScholasticJBoss service
2. Shut down ScholasticMySQL sevice
3. Run third-party software that performs backup. Configure this software to backup the **<install-drive>\ScholasticEE** directory and ALL subdirectories.
4. Start up ScholasticMySQL
5. Start up ScholasticJBoss

APPENDIX B: FOLDER STRUCTURES

Appendix B1: SAM Server folders

Folder or subfolder	Description
Top (Root) Directory of Hard Drive	Example: C:\ or MyMacHardDrive/
\ScholasticEE	The topmost directory that holds SAM Server. The name of this directory is customizable during installation, hence the name may be different. For example, if the user running the installer decided to not use the default path, and instead put the SAM Server at "C:\MySchoolSAM," the "ScholasticEE" directory name would be REPLACED BY the name "MySchoolSAM."
\SAM_Server	Holds ALL SAM Server files, including the database. This directory name and all subdirectories are fixed, not customizable by the installation process. This directory also includes installer log files.
\backup	Installation-based backups. Each time the SAM Server is upgraded, a new subdirectory is created and a backup of the database (MySQL) and server (JBoss) is placed here. The current time is used to create the subdirectory in the form of YYMMDDhhmmss.
\java	Installer support file
\jboss	The JBoss server
\server\lycea\deploy\backup.war	Database backup files created by using the SAM Client Backup process accessed through Advanced Settings.
\server\lycea\log	JBoss server log files. These log files contain information, warning, and error messages produced by the JBoss server. Log entries are written to the server.log file; every 24 hours the server.log file is moved to server.log. [time-stamp], and a new server.log file is started.

Folder or subfolder	Description
\log	Installer log files and JBoss standard output and error log files.
\mysql	Database directory
\data **AND** **\ibdata** **AND** **\iblogs**	These three directories contain ALL SAM Server database data.
\data	Contains error files for localhost and machine-name files.
\support\AIDA32	Windows only. AIDA32 is a program that analyzes a machine and reports on all hardware and installed software components. For problem machines, this program is used to generate an electronic report to be sent to Scholastic. See the appendix section of this document for how to use AIDA32.
\util	Utilities for supporting SAM Server
ScholasticMySQL	Mac OS X only. Contains database startup and shutdown script
ScholasticJBoss	Mac OS X only. Contains JBoss server startup and shutdown scripts.

Appendix B2: SAM Client Workstation folders

Folder or subfolder	Description
Top (Root) Directory of Hard Drive	Example: C:\ or MyMacHardDrive/
\Program Files	Windows only: General location that holds application programs
\Applications	Mac OS X and Classic only: General location that holds application programs
\Scholastic Enterprise	Holds all Scholastic Enterprise Edition client applications. Also contains installation log files.
\SRI	Scholastic Reading Inventory (SRI) Client
\support\AIDA32	Windows only. AIDA32 is a program that analyzes a machine and reports on all hardware and installed software components. For problem machines, this program is used to generate an electronic report to be sent to Scholastic. See the appendix section of this document for how to use AIDA32.

APPENDIX C: DATA MOVEMENT TEMPLATES AND DATA POINTS

Appendix C1: Data Movement Data Points

Use this chart to determine which data points will transfer during any of the data movement activities.

		Migration	Aggregation	CSV or XML Roster Import	Student Transfer	Backup
SAM Roster Data	Last Name	X	X	X	X	X
	Middle Initial	X	X	X	X	X
	First Name	X	X	X	X	X
	Student ID	X	X	X	X	X
	Username	X	X	X	X	X
	Password	X	X	X	X	X
	Other ID	X	X	X	X	X
	Gender	X	X	X	X	X
	Ethnicity	X	X	X	X	X
	Grade	X	X	X	X	X
	Economically Disadvantaged	X	X	X	X	X
	Limited English Proficiency	X	X	X	X	X
	Gifted and Talented	X	X	X	X	X
	Students with Disabilities	X	X	X	X	X
	Migrant	X	X	X	X	X
	Special Ed (SMS Only)	X	X	X	X	X
	Custom AYP Subgroup Info		X		X	X
	School structure		X			X
	Licensing data					X
	Product controls and settings					X
SRI	Most Recent Lexile	X	X		X	X
	Most Recent Percentile Rank		X		X	X
	Most Recent NCE		X		X	X
	Most Recent Test Date	X	X		X	X
	All Performance Data	X	X		X	X

Appendix C2: XML template

Use this template as a model for any *.xml files you wish to import. (The names and student information provided in this template are only examples.)


```
<?xml version="1.0" encoding="UTF-8" ?>
- <EXPORT_DATA>
  - <ROW>
      <USER_NAME>ChristineBracco</USER_NAME>
      <PASSWORD>CB100</PASSWORD>
      <SIS_ID>10001</SIS_ID>
      <FIRST_NAME>Christine</FIRST_NAME>
      <LAST_NAME>Bracco</LAST_NAME>
      <MIDDLE_NAME />
      <GRADE>7</GRADE>
      <ETHNIC_CAUCASIAN>Y</ETHNIC_CAUCASIAN>
      <ETHNIC_AFRICAN_AM>N</ETHNIC_AFRICAN_AM>
      <ETHNIC_HISPANIC>N</ETHNIC_HISPANIC>
      <ETHNIC_PACIFIC_ISL>N</ETHNIC_PACIFIC_ISL>
      <ETHNIC_AM_IND_AK_NATIVE>N</ETHNIC_AM_IND_AK_NATIVE>
      <ETHNIC_ASIAN>N</ETHNIC_ASIAN>
      <GENDER_MALE>N</GENDER_MALE>
      <GENDER_FEMALE>Y</GENDER_FEMALE>
      <AYP_ECON_DISADVANTAGED>N</AYP_ECON_DISADVANTAGED>
      <AYP_LTD_ENGLISH_PROFICIENCY>N</AYP_LTD_ENGLISH_PROFICIENCY>
      <AYP_GIFTED_TALENTED>N</AYP_GIFTED_TALENTED>
      <AYP_MIGRANT>N</AYP_MIGRANT>
      <AYP_WITH_DISABILITIES>Y</AYP_WITH_DISABILITIES>
    </ROW>
  - <ROW>
      <USER_NAME>JamalEvans</USER_NAME>
      <PASSWORD />
      <SIS_ID>10002</SIS_ID>
      <FIRST_NAME>Jamal</FIRST_NAME>
      <LAST_NAME>Evans</LAST_NAME>
      <MIDDLE_NAME />
      <GRADE>8</GRADE>
      <ETHNIC_CAUCASIAN />
      <ETHNIC_AFRICAN_AM />
      <ETHNIC_HISPANIC />
      <ETHNIC_PACIFIC_ISL />
      <ETHNIC_AM_IND_AK_NATIVE />
      <ETHNIC_ASIAN />
      <GENDER_MALE />
      <GENDER_FEMALE />
      <AYP_ECON_DISADVANTAGED />
      <AYP_LTD_ENGLISH_PROFICIENCY />
      <AYP_GIFTED_TALENTED />
      <AYP_MIGRANT />
      <AYP_WITH_DISABILITIES />
    </ROW>
</EXPORT_DATA>
```

Appendix C3: CSV template

The CSV template resembles a Microsoft Excel file that includes all of the following headers in the first row:

USER_NAME
PASSWORD
SIS_ID
FIRST_NAME
LAST_NAME
MIDDLE_NAME
GRADE
ETHNIC_CAUCASIAN
ETHNIC_AFRICAN_AM
ETHNIC_HISPANIC
ETHNIC_PACIFIC_ISL
ETHNIC_AM_IND_AK_NATIVE
ETHNIC_ASIAN
GENDER_MALE
GENDER_FEMALE
AYP_ECON_DISADVANTAGED
AYP_LTD_ENGLISH_PROFICIENCY
AYP_GIFTED_TALENTED
AYP_MIGRANT
AYP_WITH DISABILITIES

Student information is represented in successive rows after the headers.

APPENDIX D: STARTING AND STOPPING SERVICES

Both ScholasticMySQL (a database engine) and ScholasticJBoss: JSEE (http) server are installed by SAM. Starting and stopping them will not affect other non-SAM services.

The server applications will start after the initial installation, and also each time the machine boots up. It should therefore be unnecessary for you to start the server application manually.

To stop services:
You must stop JBoss first, wait approximately 10 seconds and then stop MySQL.

Windows:

1. Log in as administrator.
2. Go to **Start → Settings → Control Panel → Administrative Tools → Services**
3. In list, look for ScholasticMySQL and ScholasticJBoss
4. Stop services by right-clicking on service, and selecting the **Stop** button.

Mac OS X:

1. Open → **Applications** → **Utilities** → **Terminal**
2. Type: 'sudo /Library/StartupItems/ScholasticJBoss/ScholasticJBoss stop'
3. Type: 'sudo /Library/StartupItems/ScholasticJBoss/ScholasticMySQL stop'

To start services:

You must start the ScholasticMySQL service first, then wait about 10 seconds before starting the ScholasticJBoss service. The ScholasticJBoss service can take up to 5 minutes to start on older machines.

Windows:

1. Log in as administrator.
2. Go to **Start → Settings → Control Panel → Administrative Tools → Services**
3. In list, look for ScholasticMySQL and ScholasticJBoss
4. Start services by right-clicking on service, and selecting the **Start** button.

You will know that the services are running correctly if you can access the SAM EE system via the SAM Client.

As an alternative to using the GUI Administrative Services screen, you can also use the Windows command line as follows:

```
net start ScholasticMySQL
net start ScholasticJBoss
```

Mac OS X

Each server application has a startup item/startup script.

1. Open → **Applications → Utilities → Terminal**
2. Type: 'sudo /Library/StartupItems/ScholasticMySQL/ScholasticMySQL start'
3. Type: 'sudo /Library/StartupItems/ScholasticJBoss/ScholasticJBoss start'

APPENDIX E: REPORTS FOR SCHOLASTIC TECHNICAL SERVICES

Using AIDA32 to create a Windows Hardware/Software Configuration Report:

In the event that an installation problem involving any version of Windows OS requires support from the Scholastic Education Technology Group (SETG), the AIDA32 program should be run to produce a hardware and software configuration report for the problematic workstation(s) and server(s). This report should then be sent to SETG as part of the problem-submission process.

1. Start the AIDA32 program
    a. The AIDA32 program is located in three locations:
        i. On the SRI Client CD, under the directory: <CD-Drive>\Support\AIDA32
        ii. On the Windows workstation hard drive where the programs are located (e.g., C:\Program Files\Scholastic Enterprise\Support\AIDA32)
        iii. On the Windows Server hard drive where the database is located:
        (e.g., <network-drive>\SCHSUITE\Support\AIDA32)
    b. In any location, simply double-click the **aida32.exe** executable to start the program.

    Upon startup:

    The first screen will be titled "AIDA32—Enterprise System Information." A navigation bar will exist along the left side of the screen. A component-information screen will exist in the middle and right side of the screen.

General system analysis:

By selecting different left-navigation items (e.g., Computer [summary information], Operating System, Network, Software, etc.), and then selecting sub-items, the middle-right screen will display that item's information.

- Example: Click **Computer**, then click **Summary** to obtain a summary of all hardware and software components on the machine.
- Example: Click **Motherboard**, then click **CPU** to obtain detailed information on the CPU for the machine.

2. To generate a report:
   a. Click the top-navigation bar's Report menu.
   b. Click **Report Wizard**.
   c. Click **Next** to accept the welcome screen.
   d. On the **Report Profiles** screen, select the option based on type of system error being resolved.
      i. For general error resolution, select **System Summary Only.**
      ii. If you suspect hardware problems, run a report with the **System Summary Only**, and also another report with **Hardware-Related Pages.**
      iii. If DLL problems, run the report with **All Pages** selected.
         - Note: **All Pages** will take upwards of 30 minutes to run on older systems. This produces valuable information but requires detailed analysis of all DLL's and other low-level system information analysis.
         - In general, this is the most useful of all reports.
   e. Select **Plain Text** for Report Format.
   f. After the report is produced, select **Save To File**, and save to a temporary place.

3. Send the report to Scholastic.

Creating an Apple System Profiler to Gather Macintosh Machine Information

In the event that an installation problem involving any version of Macintosh requires support from the Scholastic Education Technology Group (SETG), you should use the Apple provided **System Profiler** utility program to produce a hardware and software configuration report for the problematic workstation(s) and/or server(s). This report should then be sent to SETG as part of the problem-submission process.

Mac OS X

1. Click the **Apple** icon in upper-left corner of desktop and click **About this Mac.**
2. Click the **More Info** button.
3. On top menu bar, click **File** then **Save As.**
4. Select **Plain Text** in the drop-down for **File Format.**
5. Name the file and save it to a location of your choice by clicking **Save.**
6. Send the saved text document to Scholastic.

Mac Classic 9.2

1. Click the **Apple** icon in the upper-left corner.
2. Click **Apple System Profiler** in the drop-down list.
3. On top menu bar, click **File** then **New Report.**
4. A pop-up window will appear. Click all check boxes (including the ones on the right side), then click **OK**. If a pop-up states the report is too large to be viewed in a text document, simply click **OK**.
5. A new pop-up window will appear, listing the system profile information. Click the radio button for **TEXT DOCUMENT.**
6. On the top menu bar, click **File**, then **Save As**; name the file and save it to a location of your choice by clicking **Save.**
7. Send the saved text document to Scholastic.

APPENDIX F: PORTS AND THEIR USES

Port Numbers and Their Uses

Port numbers are used by processes/programs on a computer to talk to other processes/programs on the same computer and, in certain cases to accept communication calls from external computers. There are approximately 65,000 ports available on all machines for this type of communication. The SAM EE Server requires 8 port numbers to correctly process—one of which is used to communicate between clients and the SAM Server. The default ports used with their descriptions are:

55880—Application Server

- Used to communicate with the client applications. This communication is HTTP, the standard for Internet communication.
- The standard ports for HTTP servers are 80 and 8080. We change this port value to prevent conflict with any pre-existing HTTP servers, such as a school's Intranet Web server.
- This is the ONLY port that requires access from other machines (e.g., the client applications). Hence, this port number MUST be allowed in any firewall or proxy a school has set up.

55881—AJP

55882—JNDI

55883—Database

- Used for the HTTP server (JBoss) to communicate to the MySQL database.
- In standard MySQL installations, this is set to port number 3306. We change the port value to avoid conflict with any pre-existing MySQL database. This allows other non-SAM EE (and non-Scholastic) MySQL databases to run on the same server.

55884—Pooled

55885—RMI

55886—RMIObject

55887—Web Service

During installation, any or all of these ports can be changed by the user by clicking **Edit** at the first **Port Summary** screen to manually set each value, or by the installers if one of these default ports is already in use by some other service or program. In the event that the **Application Server** port number (default 55880) changes, then the changed value is what must be used to configure all clients and for firewall and proxy changes.

Also note that all manually set port numbers must be greater than 1024; numbers at and below 1024 are generally reserved and have OS level security to prevent their usage without specific Administrative or Root privileges.

APPENDIX G: UNINSTALLING SAM AND SERVER COMPONENTS

IMPORTANT NOTE: There are no automatic SAM Server uninstallers, as uninstalling SAM will result in a loss of all data. A system administrator or someone with similar skills should be the only person to perform uninstallation.

Windows: Uninstalling SAM Server and Server Components

1. Stop the ScholasticMySQL and ScholasticJBoss services.

   Each application can be shut down through the service mechanism, either through the services control panel or from the command line.

   At the **Control Panel**:

   1. Click **Administrative Tools.**
   2. Click **Services.**
   3. Under the **Name** column:
      i. Select **ScholasticJBoss**, right-click, then choose **Stop service.**
      ii. Select **ScholasticMySQL**, right-click, then choose **Stop service.**

   Alternatively:

   - Windows 2000, select **Start → Run** and type **cmd.exe.**
   - Windows 2003 or XP, select **Start → Command Prompt.**
   - Then, at the command line type:
      i. net stop ScholasticJBoss
      ii. net stop ScholasticMySQL

2. Remove the ScholasticMySQL and ScholasticJBoss services.

   The easiest way is to use the MySQL daemon to remove each service using the Windows command line:

      i. cd <install directory>/mysql/bin
      ii. mysql d—remove ScholasticJBoss
      iii. mysql d—remove ScholasticMySQL

3. Remove the installation directory.

   Using Windows Explorer, select the **SAM_Server** directory and delete it. If there are no other Scholastic sub-directories under the **ScholasticEE** directory, then you can also delete the **ScholasticEE** directory.

You may now uninstall the Scholastic program Clients, using the Windows uninstall feature.

Mac OS X: Uninstalling SAM and Server Components

1. Stop the ScholasticMySQL and ScholasticJBoss services.

   Each server application has a startup item/startup script through which the application can be shut down. Open a Terminal (/Applications/Utilities/Terminal) window and run:

   1. sudo /Library/StartupItems/ScholasticMySQL/ScholasticMySQL stop
   2. sudo /Library/StartupItems/ScholasticJBoss/ScholasticJBoss stop

2. Remove the ScholasticMySQL and ScholasticJBoss services.

   Provided in the installation is a script to accomplish this:

   1. cd <install directory>/util
   2. sudo ./startup_items.sh uninstall

   If you have already removed the installation directory, you can remove the items manually by:

   1. sudo rm -rf /Library/StartupItems/Scholastic*

3. Remove the additional user and groups for Mac OS X.

   The installer adds a user 'samadmin' and a group 'schlgrp' to your system. To remove these, a script is provided. Open a Terminal (/Applications/Utilities/Terminal) window and run:

   1. cd <install directory>/util
   2. sudo ./adduser.sh uninstall

   If you want to remove the user and group and have already removed the installation directory, you can remove them manually by:

   1. sudo niutil destroy / /users/samadmin
   2. sudo niutil destroy / /users/schlgrp

You may now uninstall the Scholastic program Clients.

CONTACTS

To learn more about ***SRI:***

SRI Web site: ***www.scholastic.com/sri***

To inquire about ***SRI***, purchase or activate licenses, or track shipped materials:

Customer Service: 1-877-COUNTS1 (268-6871) 7:00 A.M.–6:00 P.M. (CST)

Direct email address: **sri@scholastic.com**

To get technical support:

Technical Support: 1-800-283-5974 7:00 A.M.–8:00 P.M. (EST)

Navigate from ***www.scholastic.com/sri*** to technical support email, chat, and FAQs.